PORTRAIT OF WI

Poet and Soldier, 1893—1918

by

HELEN M^CPHAIL

G L I D D O N   B O O K S
in association with
THE WILFRED OWEN ASSOCIATION

First published 1993 by Gliddon Books
and The Wilfred Owen Association

Printed by Strand Press, Petersfield, Hampshire

© Helen McPhail, 1993
Bibliography, © David Hughes, 1993

ISBN 0 947893318

Map of Great Britain, showing
towns mentioned in the text.

Contents

Introduction

'This book is not about heroes. English poetry is not yet
fit to speak of them.
Nor is it about deeds, or lands, nor anything about glory,
honour, might, majesty, dominion, or power, except
War.
Above all I am not concerned with Poetry.
My subject is War, and the pity of War.
The Poetry is in the pity.
Yet these elegies are to this generation in no sense
consolatory. They may be to the next. All a poet can do
today is warn. That is why the true Poets must be
truthful.'

From Wilfred Owen's draft Preface for a collection of
war poems that he was preparing for publication in 1919.

'. . . it is the preface, by Wilfred Owen, to a volume of
his poems which was to show, to England, and the
intolerant world, the foolishness, unnaturalness, horror,
inhumanity, and insupportability of war, and to expose,
so that all could suffer and see, the heroic lies, the
willingness of the old to sacrifice the young,
indifference, grief, the soul of soldiers. . . he is a poet of
all times, all places, and all wars. There is only one war:
that of men against men.'

Dylan Thomas

The war of 1914-1918 has receded into history. We are left with
family memories and great quantities of history books and
published memoirs — but virtually no one, now, to tell us in
person what it felt like to be a soldier of the Great War.

Quite apart from its many social and military upheavals, it
was a literary war, in a way that no other war had been before
or perhaps will be again, with thousands of men and women
recording their impressions in print. A few writers found a style
which is in sympathy with the disillusioned attitudes of later
generations and Wilfred Owen is one of those whose writing
remains vivid and convincing: through his poems and letters we
learn the truth about war, and the pity of war.

Fascinated by poetry and its power from a young age, Owen
fixed his ambitions on writing poetry through a self-imposed
apprenticeship in the use of language that fitted him for his

experience of war. Faced with the challenges of life and death in the trenches, Owen respected the men in his charge and insists that we understand what happened to them: the poems and the letters tell us the truth and the way in which he tells it convinces us.

Some aspects of Owen's own life remain difficult to assess and these are discussed in the final chapter. Wilfred's brother Harold wrote his memoirs, which I have drawn on with caution, but they nonetheless present a vivid picture of a family living in modest circumstances, in the distant beginnings of the twentieth century.

Now, without everyday encounters to explain or recall the First World War and its times, we must trust the poets to help us see their experiences and feelings from the inside. Owen's letters are revealing, vigorous, convincing, his poems deeply moving in their directness and honesty. Killed on 4 November 1918 — so poignantly near to the end of the Great War — he nevertheless still has much to tell us as inhabitants of the late twentieth century world.

Following the Trail

The aim of this book is to present a brief outline of Wilfred Owen's life. More detailed information and literary analysis is widely available (see Bibliography, p. 75), but the maps given here make it possible to follow Owen's movements in France with accuracy for the first time; exploring the landscapes of the First World War offers a deeper understanding of the poet's voice.

Despite the passage of three-quarters of a century it is still possible to revisit the past. English city centres may have been rebuilt but the quiet Victorian streets where the Owens rented their various houses have changed little; Oswestry and Shrewsbury have expanded, Birkenhead has lost much of its shipping — but Wilfred would have no difficulty in recognising Shrewsbury's fine Victorian Gothic station where his father reigned and where his brother Harold saw him off after their final meeting. Both Shropshire towns now have memorials to Owen, unveiled in his centenary year of 1993.

In Ripon, the neat little cottage in Borrage Lane has long outlived the military camp, in Scarborough the Clarence Gardens Hotel — now the Clifton — still stands proudly on its cliff-top, and in Edinburgh, Craiglockhart War Hospital has changed its name, décor and purposes, but can still be admired on the edge of the city.

In France the little towns and villages of the Ancre and Somme Valleys were rebuilt after the 1918 Armistice, the trenches filled in and the farmland restored. Yet the countryside is virtually unchanged, and it is not difficult to follow the movements of the British troops between 1914 and 1918. Despite the enormous efforts put into clearing the debris of war, the land itself still reveals traces of its savage past: many fields and hillsides still show white patches of chalk brought to the surface by shell-fire, mining or trenches and curly metal picket stakes can still be seen round fields, as useful for modern farm fencing as for their original purpose of holding defensive wire. Lethal reminders of the First World War still come to the surface; an appreciable tonnage of shells is dug up each year and left by the roadside to be dealt with by experts. They are dangerous and should never be touched. Other more harmless relics are often visible — buttons, fragments of shrapnel, the occasional bit of boot or buckle.

In Ors there is a small plinth and plaque by the canal bridge, commemorating the men who fought there in November 1918. Wilfred Owen is the only individual named on it, and it bears four lines from his poem *With an Identity Disc*. It stands close to the village's own war memorial. Otherwise there is little there to recall the Great War — except for the two British military cemeteries, rows of white gravestones over the men who were killed there. One is close to the canal and reached across a field while the other, with Owen and some fifty other men lying in it, is in a corner of the village cemetery.

The most convenient general touring map for following Owen's movements in France is number 4 (Laon-Arras) in the IGN 'Serie Verte' (green) 1:100 000 series. For a more detailed approach, whether on paper, by car or on foot, the blue IGN 1:25 000 series is invaluable; modern roads in the areas covered by this book generally still follow routes used in 1914-18.

Acknowledgements

New material has appeared recently that relates directly to Wilfred Owen and I have been able, with help, to identify places of importance in his military career which make it possible to follow him with complete accuracy for the first time. I am very grateful to a number of people for their patience, interest and guidance.

Martin Taylor of the Imperial War Museum generously allowed me to use a diary discovered by him, written by one of Owen's fellow soldiers, which describes the approach to the trenches in January 1917 and clarifies Wilfred Owen's movements in April 1917. Among the members of the Wilfred Owen Association who have given their support to this book, read my manuscript and made valuable suggestions and corrections, I would particularly like to thank Dominic Hibberd and Philip Guest for their unfailing help and expert knowledge. The mayors and citizens of Ors and Joncourt have received English visitors with great courtesy, interest and helpfulness and I hope that future visitors will build upon this good relationship.

Acknowledgements and thanks are due to Oxford University Press for permission to quote from Wilfred Owen's letters; to the Trustees of the Owen Estate for permission to reproduce the photographs of Wilfred Owen on the cover and page 18; to Mrs. Pat Denny for her father's map of Ors and photograph of the original cross on Owen's grave; to Gabrielle Collins for the photograph of Craiglockhart; to Shropshire Records and Research for the photographs of the Owen family and of Shrewsbury Station. The 1918 map of Joncourt is reproduced by kind permission of the Trustees of The Manchester Regiment Collection of The King's Regiment; the Trustees of the copyrights of the late Dylan Thomas and Messrs. J. M. Dent for permission to quote from Dylan Thomas's radio talk, *Wilfred Owen*; the quotation from *A Hope for Poetry* is printed by permission of the Peters Fraser and Dunlop Group Ltd. and the Estate of C. Day Lewis; and the extract from *Heroes' Twilight* is quoted by permission of Bernard Bergonzi.

The bibliography prepared by David Hughes will undoubtedly be of great value to students of the First World War in its range of critical guidance which I could not hope to achieve on my own.

For historical information relating to the First World War, the Commonwealth War Graves Commission in Maidenhead and the Imperial War Museum in London are unique in their expertise; and for anyone interested in the modern French approach to the First World War, the museum opened in 1992 in Péronne (the *Historial de la Grande Guerre*) welcomes visitors and explains all its material in English and German as well as French.

Some dates in Wilfred Owen's life

1893   **18 March:** born, Plas Wilmot, Oswestry

1895   **16 May:** Mary Millard Owen born

1897   Plas Wilmot sold
5 September: Harold Owen born, Shrewsbury

1898   Move to Birkenhead

1900   **11 June:** Wilfred Owen starts school
24 July: Colin Shaw Owen born

1907   The Owen family moves to Shrewsbury
Wilfred Owen joins Shrewsbury Technical School

1910   **January:** move to Mahim, Monkmoor Road, Shrewsbury

1911   **October:** Wilfred Owen joins Revd. Herbert Wigan, vicar of
Dunsden, as lay assistant

1913   **February:** ill, leaves Dunsden for good
September: to Bordeaux, teaching English in Bordeaux and
the Pyrenees

1915   **September:** returns to England
15 October: Joins up, Artists' Rifles; meets Harold Munro,
Poetry Bookshop; training

1916   **4 June:** commissioned, Manchester Regiment, 5th (Reserve)
Battalion
June—August: Witley, Aldershot, Farnborough
September—Christmas: Oswestry, Southport, Fleetwood.
Embarkation leave

1917   **January:** to France, Etaples, Beaumont Hamel. In action;
holds dug-out in no man's land.
February: to Abbeville, transport course
March: rejoins battalion; evacuated following concussion
April: rejoins battalion; in action, Savy; brigade relieved
May: evacuated, shell-shock
June: Etretat, Netley, Craiglockhart War Hospital,
Edinburgh
July: visited by Susan Owen; contributes to *The Hydra*,
becomes editor
August: meets Siegfried Sassoon
October: meets Robert Graves; leaves hospital
November: meets Arnold Bennett, H. G. Wells; rejoins 5th
Manchester, Scarborough
December: promoted Lieutenant

Prelude to Fame

A dark wet November morning in 1918, at the extreme eastern point of the triumphant Allied advance across Northern France. Overhead, a monstrous deafening roar of artillery barrage. On the ground, in the fields between the village road and the canal, men waiting, quiet and tense, for the signal to advance.

The young officer at the head of one of the leading companies had recently distinguished himself in battle. Proud to have been recommended for the Military Cross, 2nd Lieutenant Wilfred Owen was confident in his men and his own abilities: their trust and affection was probably more important to him than the public recognition of his bravery. Perhaps some lines of his own poems helped to fill the moments of waiting.

The 2nd Battalion of the Manchester Regiment was on the edge of Ors, a small village in north-eastern France; it was part of the British Fourth Army driving the Germans back towards their original frontiers. On this bleak autumn morning the British task was to cross the formidable obstacle of the Sambre-Oise canal, with German units dominating the eastern bank and determined to keep it. Flanked by men of the Lancashire Fusiliers to their left and the Dorsetshire Regiment to their right, the Manchesters were to give covering fire while men of the Royal Engineers assembled a floating bridge on the water for the

---

1918   **January:** attends Graves's marriage, London; *Miners* published in *The Nation* (first national publication of any poem)
March: posted to Ripon
April: home leave, last meeting with Harold Owen
May: meets Osbert Sitwell
June: Rejoins 5th Manchester, Scarborough; Edith and Osbert Sitwell request poems for *Wheels 1918; The Nation* publishes *Hospital Barge* and *Futility*; Colin Owen joins the R.A.F.
August: Embarkation leave in London; to Etaples
September: Rejoins 5th Manchesters at Amiens; in action, Beaurevoir-Fonsomme; awarded MC
October: rest period, Hancourt; into line again. Battalion takes over line west of canal near Ors
4 November: killed in action
11 November: news of death reaches Shrewsbury.

The original cross on Wilfred Owen's grave, photographed by Lt. John Foulkes after the war.

troops to cross the canal and re-form, ready to advance further. Withdrawal was not part of the plan.

They advanced as instructed to the top of the bank and the sappers got to work as the Germans opened fire. The British troops were all in the German line of fire now, from machine guns on the rising ground beyond the canal.

It was a fierce engagement, shatteringly noisy and intense, the first active combat in an area which had been occupied and firmly controlled by the invading enemy since the frantic movement of 1914. The Germans too had no intention of withdrawing.

Owen and his men directed their fire across the canal as the Royal Engineers strained purposefully, struggling with the bridging equipment by the canal waters. The engagement was fierce and shatteringly noisy as enemy machine-gun bullets tore into them and the casualties were heavy. Close to Owen a young subaltern calmly ferried his Lewis gun out on to the canal, into the heart of the battle, and gave covering fire.

Steady throughout the turmoil, Owen guided and encouraged his men with a comforting hand and word in the furious melée. He was last seen on a raft on the canal. By 7 a.m. — still barely full day in the gloom of a November dawn and the swirling gas and mist — the operation was called off and Wilfred Owen was among the dead.

A child of Victorian rural England, he had travelled far in mind and body in his brief quarter-century of life.

1. Growing Up

Wilfred Owen was born on 18 March 1893, into middle-class stability and comfort in Oswestry, a busy market town in the remote and beautiful Welsh border country of Shropshire. His parents, Tom and Susan Owen, lived in Susan's family home with her father Edward Shaw, a prosperous businessman and former mayor.

Tom Owen's family was Welsh in origin, but his parents had lived in Nantwich before settling in Shrewsbury where his father was employed in one of the town's largest shops. Before his marriage Tom, a railway clerk, spent several years in India; working his passage out gave him an enduring regret at leaving the sea, but he was successful and happy in his Indian railways job. News from the Shaw family that Susan's young brother Edward — a youthful football-playing companion — had fallen into dissolute ways and drunkenness brought Tom back to Oswestry, marriage and the railway company there instead of waiting for Susan to join him in India. Edward disappeared to the United States and was never heard of again, a disgrace to his prosperous family.

Susan continued to keep house for her father until his death in 1897. Life changed then for the young Owens, for the old man had been living beyond his means: his daughter and son-in-law had to sell the quiet substantial house and move to considerably more modest surroundings in Birkenhead, where Tom found a better paid railway job. Wilfred, their first child, was born in his grandfather's house in Oswestry, followed by Mary in 1895, Harold in 1897 and Colin in 1900.

Between 1897 and 1906 the Owens lived in three different houses in the Tranmere district of Birkenhead. (The houses still exist — 7 Elm Grove, 14 Willmer Road and 51 Milton Road.[1]) Despite the tone of *Journey from Obscurity*, the memoirs written by Wilfred's brother Harold in his prosperous later years, these were not slum streets; but they were distinctly less imposing than the house in Oswestry and no doubt encouraged Susan's nostalgia for the comforts and security of her childhood. The family's limited financial resources still stretched to maid-servants, and music lessons for the children, however, as Susan

[1] Recent investigation (1993) of electoral rolls has shown that this is the correct sequence of addresses.

Shrewsbury Station, photographed in 1903.

insisted on the family's respectability and proper appearances.

Harold records some vivid memories of childhood, with Wilfred frequently in charge of the younger children. His position as eldest of the family and his mother's tendency to favour him helped to make the brothers' relationship an uneasy one — and Wilfred was evidently inclined from an early age to a serious-minded and anxiously authoritative attitude which did not endear him to his juniors. Mary, although older than Harold, was physically tiny and frail and seems to have been loved but largely disregarded by the brothers.

The Birkenhead years covered the period of Wilfred's early education, at Birkenhead Institute, and also a variety of enjoyable holidays. Tom Owen's supervisory post with the GW and LNWR Railways brought with it free rail passes which were put to good use by the whole family; they all travelled to Ireland more than once and Susan went on frequent visits to her sisters in London and later Reading. The pattern of her movements can be seen from the many letters that Wilfred wrote to her, keeping her up to date with family activities and his own school life. Another significant holiday during this period was the fortnight spent by Susan and Wilfred alone at Broxton in the Cheshire hills when he was 10 or 11 — both Harold and Wilfred himself later identified this as a moment when he began to think of poetry as a means of expression and self-fulfilment.

The winter of 1906-7 brought a further major upheaval for the Owens: Tom was appointed Assistant Superintendent for the railways' Western Region, a promotion which meant moving to Shrewsbury.

The Owens first rented 1 Cleveland Place, Underdale Road, and then three years later (in 1910) they moved to a slightly larger house, 'Mahim', in Monkmoor Road. The two houses are not far apart, tall, solid and plain, late Victorian, close to Shrewsbury Abbey and the Technical School which Wilfred attended. Mary attended a small private school while Harold scrambled and fought his way unsatisfactorily through a series of Shrewsbury elementary schools.

The family's leisure time was occupied with a variety of outdoor explorings, on foot or bicycle, urged on by Tom who was active and gregarious. A letter from Wilfred to his youngest brother Colin in 1909 describes a long bicycle ride to The Wrekin — the distinctive hill in eastern Shropshire — and to Uriconium, the ancient Roman city outside Shrewsbury which fascinated Wilfred. He often visited the site, digging about and uncovering Roman remains on several occasions and one of his juvenile poems, written in 1913, is concerned with Uriconium and the area's remote history. A feeling for the beautiful Shropshire countryside and the hidden weight of the past lies behind much of his later work and, although the Owens always lived in urban surroundings, the landscape of rural England was clearly important to Wilfred's imagination.

Susan, meanwhile, suffering — and perhaps exploiting — poor

'Mahim', the Owens' house in Monkmoor Road, Shrewsbury, with a plaque over the door commemorating Wilfred Owen. The attic window belongs to his bedroom, from which he had a good view over open country to Haughmond Hill.

13

health, encouraged Wilfred to remain with her or at his books. She seems to have had few interests outside her family and the Church and most of her maternal energy seems to have been devoted to stimulating her eldest son's talents and devotion to her — indeed, her concentration on his welfare was so intense that, decades later, she still spoke only of Wilfred and friends heard nothing of Mary, Harold or Colin. Wilfred's natural studiousness was encouraged by Susan's attitude; the impression given both by Wilfred's references to Tom Owen in his letters and by Harold in his memoirs — even allowing for the inevitable and unconscious distortions from writing many decades later — is of two somewhat disappointed parents and divisions within the family. An image emerges from various memoirs and letters of an unsophisticated, active, conventional and rather restricted household. Baulked in any ambitions she may have had for her husband's worldly success, Susan was concerned to keep up proper appearances: photographs always show them smartly dressed and Wilfred was undoubtedly very conscious of his appearance and clothes. Above all it was important to avoid the threat of sliding into working-class poverty which had seemed an alarming possibility in Birkenhead.

When the family moved to Shrewsbury there was a suggestion that Wilfred should remain in Birkenhead, living with his great friend Alec Paton and continuing to attend Birkenhead Institute where he had made an excellent start. This was not acceptable to Susan, however, and he continued his education at the Technical School in Shrewsbury (now rebuilt as the Wakeman School), close to the River Severn and not far from home. Although he made few close friends he was popular with his teachers and plunged into English literature, history, poetry, drama, classical legends, French, archaeology, botany... Delighting in his own language, Wilfred revelled in Shakespeare and the English Romantic poets; Shelley and above all Keats became his literary idols and models. He enjoyed the whole process of learning, which included two highly successful holidays with his father in Brittany, in 1908 and 1909. Father and son alone together on a foreign holiday seem to have been more at ease with each other than in their everyday Shrewsbury surroundings.

Despite his application, however, he did not always shine as he would have liked and a letter in 1910 records his disappointment at not coming top (and also his delight in school sports):

> 'F. Watson remains impregnable! for all my exam successes, (e.g. French 91, History 94), her army of Term Marks she so diligently has mustered are superior to mine... We (boys) are all working away in Recreation Time... mowing and rolling 2 Tennis Courts. I hope to play soon, may I? Already I have had some cricket there. Hockey and Football go on at the same time! Isn't it a marvellous outburst!'

At around this time — aged 17 — he was writing some of the earliest poems to have survived; *To Poesy* and *Written in a Wood, September 1910* both show the strength of his admiration for Keats.

Church attendance was important for the whole family, with Bible reading and Evangelical faith to the fore, under Susan's determined guidance; and although in later years Wilfred fell out of sympathy with the Church, the language and teaching of the Bible and the Book of Common Prayer are often apparent in his work. Their favourite place of worship came to be the quiet church in Uffington, a small village which they reached by walking down through the meadows close to home and taking a rope-hauled ferry across the River Severn.

When he left school at 18 — having been allowed to stay on beyond the standard leaving age despite his family's modest finances — Wilfred knew that the university education he longed for was not available without a scholarship. Teaching seemed an obvious and suitable profession — but his headmaster's wife made a special visit to warn him against the grind and tedium of elementary teaching and a short spell in the Wyle Cop elementary school in Shrewsbury confirmed this advice. Depressed and uncertain at his failure to achieve honours in the University of London matriculation examination — his hoped-for route to the literary future which was his true ambition — he agreed to become an unpaid lay assistant to an Evangelical vicar near Reading in return for further academic coaching. He left home in October 1911.

2. Independence

The venture was not a success. Susan's ambition for her favourite son to enter the Church was frustrated as Wilfred grew disenchanted with the atmosphere of arid religiosity that he found in the vicarage at Dunsden, a few miles from Reading. Matters were not helped by the Reverend Herbert Wigan's unwillingness to tutor Wilfred as arranged; the young lay assistant's time was fully taken up with parish duties.

Many aspects of these duties were enjoyable, however, and there was much to be learned from observation of village life and the problems of rural poverty. Understanding of human problems and sympathy for the victims of ignorance, wretched living conditions and ill health can be seen in Wilfred's letters and poems of the period. The poems that survive reflect the influence of Keats, as ever, and adolescent gloom, but also — as in *Deep under Turfy Grass* (inspired by the double funeral of a mother and her young daughter) — deep feeling for other people's distress which showed a capacity for sympathy as well as for observation. As Wilfred's enthusiasm for the Church waned he sought intellectual activity in classes at Reading University; here he met an understanding English teacher who offered him helpful advice on his reading.

The high points of Wilfred's time at Dunsden were a holiday in Scotland with his family in July 1912, and the friendships he developed with children in the parish. However, these personal friendships with the young pupils were frowned upon by the vicar. Desperate to continue his study of the English poets and to increase his own writing skills, Wilfred found himself under increasing stress as his instincts met with disapproval. In other matters his restrained and prudish home background was of little help to a confused adolescent; his poetic efforts at this time reflect a growing awareness of sexuality and the need for love combined with uncertainty and unease.

The neat and attentive pupil, the devout and devoted son was growing up. The dissatisfaction on both sides of the Dunsden vicarage dining table finally came to a head and by Christmas 1912 it was clearly time for him to leave.

To France

1913 began unpromisingly, for when Wilfred returned to Shrewsbury in February he was ill for some weeks. Apart from genuine illness, he was evidently also suffering from depression and uncertainty over his future. Tensions increased within the family when Harold, now 15, was told that he must leave school and find work; after the failures of his early school years he had discovered a talent as an artist and wanted desperately to continue with his art classes as a pupil teacher — but Tom and Susan felt they could not support two grown sons: Wilfred was not only senior in age, he automatically had first claim on the family's money and ambitions.

Harold went off to join the Merchant Navy, while Wilfred recuperated, took and failed the scholarship examination for Reading University, and looked for further occupation. In mid-September he left for France to teach English in the Berlitz School in Bordeaux, where the milder climate would be good for his health. He intended to write poetry and improve his French.

The remaining months of 1913 and the first half of 1914 passed in the laborious grind of a heavy teaching load. Wilfred enjoyed his independence, and made friends. It was with the family of one pupil that he celebrated his 21st birthday in March 1914 and with another that he went off to the Pyrenees for the summer. His letters home at this period — for he was an indefatigable letter writer, almost always to his mother — speak of minor health problems, the burdens of life as an overworked teacher, and later the delights of rural life in the Pyrenees.

Through the hot summer of 1914, Wilfred's letters paid little attention to events stirring in the wider world. He found his employers, Monsieur and Madame Léger, a thoroughly agreeable and cultured couple and their daughter Nénette a delightful child. His circumstances were improving, both socially and intellectually.

Family life with the Légers also brought him an important new friend, Laurent Tailhade: a survivor of the French Decadent poets of the 1890s, Tailhade had been a friend of Verlaine, and an active anarchist. Showing great affection for the young English teacher and aspiring poet, Tailhade extended Owen's knowledge and encouraged him to experiment with the technical structures of poetry. Owen's writing after this period shows an awareness of sound effects in general, including the first traces of 'pararhyme' (deliberate near-rhymes with matching consonants and varying vowel sounds).[2] He was getting into his stride as an adult now, ready to expand his ideas and creative style, enjoying his independence and his poetry; photographs show Wilfred with Tailhade and the Légers, a dapper young man, not tall but fit and energetic, smartly dressed with polished boots, a bow tie and soft hat, and a neatly clipped moustache.

Wilfred Owen with Madame Léger, the Pyrenees, August 1914.

Apart from stimulating company and conversations there were possible commercial ventures to be considered. Susan Owen was evidently concerned about Madame Léger, an interior designer, who suggested taking Wilfred to Canada on business, for Wilfred took some trouble to assure his mother both that Madame was entirely respectable and that he was not unsuitably involved with her; clearly the only woman in Wilfred's life continued to be his mother.

Back in Bordeaux once more he earned his living as a freelance teacher, until towards the end of 1914 he became tutor in a household with a quartet of English boys. Now his letters were more likely to refer to the war: a dismissive reference in August 1914 to guns that 'will effect a little useful weeding' was soon followed by vivid descriptions, accompanied by sketches, of soldiers' wounds and operations seen in the Bordeaux hospitals.

While the English and French armies fought desperately to stem the triumphant German advance and then found themselves at a standstill, dug into the ground in the cold and damp of Flanders and northern France, Wilfred continued to study French, teach English and consider his future. His thoughts

[2]Tailhade's influence extended to other English poets. Ezra Pound (1885-1972), the avant-garde Imagist poet, recorded his admiration for Tailhade. This was probably for his satire whereas Owen admired his more conventional elegiac poems.

were still inclined towards life as a poet — what he was to describe as 'the fullest-largest liveable life'. Apart from a brief visit to England on a commercial mission in May 1915, he did not finally return until September of that year; and by now he had made up his mind: 'I don't want to wear khaki; not yet to save my honour. . . But I *now do most intensely want to fight.*'

In Khaki

The war, originally expected to be 'all over by Christmas', had been going on for over a year now and had settled into a terrible routine of attrition along the trenches of the Western Front. The colossal Allied losses of the first few months of fighting were followed by the miserable battles and stalemate conditions of 1915 in France and Belgium and the disaster of Gallipoli.

Before leaving Bordeaux in the summer of 1915 Wilfred had written to his cousin Leslie Gunston — probably his closest friend — that he did not 'imagine that the German War will be affected by my joining in, but I know my own future Peace will be'. Now, in October, he could feel at peace with himself as he joined up, enlisting in the Artists' Rifles. This happy choice of unit enabled him to spend his first weeks of drilling practice in Bloomsbury, with its echoes of Dickens and other literary heroes. Here Wilfred met his first living English poet, Harold Monro, whose Poetry Bookshop was the haunt and delight of poets and readers alike, and who gave the young officer cadet his attention, friendship and advice.

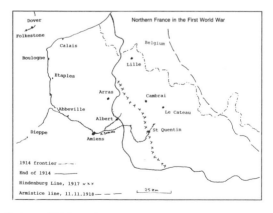

Northern France, 1914-1918.

19

After training in London and Essex; Owen was commissioned in June 1916 into the Manchester Regiment, and then continued his soldiering apprenticeship on various courses which took him to Aldershot, Southport and Fleetwood. His letters home throughout this summer are full of military trivia with no mention of the war, although British troops on the Western Front were plunged into the Battle of the Somme. His own regiment's 2nd Battalion was one of those involved in heavy fighting on the first day of the battle (1 July) which, with over 57,000 casualties, was the worst day ever suffered by the British Army. 2nd Lieutenant W. E. S. Owen was posted to this battalion in France to fill one of the many gaps created by the autumn's continued bitter fighting.

On 29 December 1916, after a hasty trip to London to see his brother Harold, Wilfred wrote home from Folkestone: 'There is a Boat at 11.30 a.m. More I know not.'

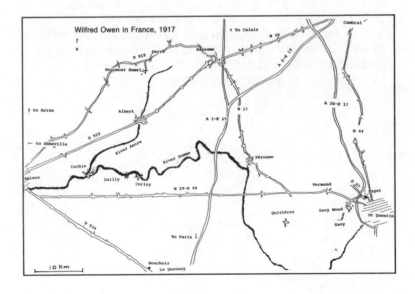

Following Owen in France, January—May 1917, showing modern main roa

3. 'Mud and Thunder'

Mud was the first hostile element, penetrating — as he put it jauntily a few days after arriving — into 'that holy of holies, my pyjamas'. Active service in France was very different from childhood holidays or the long months in Bordeaux and the Pyrenees.

The battalion which he joined on 6 January 1917 had recently suffered heavy losses near Beaumont Hamel during the Battle of the Ancre: on one November day it had gone into action over 600 strong but come out with only six officers and 150 men.

Wilfred's early letters from France must have fed his mother's usual concern for her precious son. He sent her vivid accounts of the living conditions, the difficulty of movement and the discomforts of mud everywhere and the fierce cold; it was the coldest winter for decades and the drab discomforts of camp life in England were a poor preparation for existence in ruined houses, or trenches where men could — and did — freeze to death. If Wilfred wrote any poetry in these unpromising circumstances, none of it has survived.

An enterprising soldier servant made life more bearable, for he 'keeps a jolly fire going and thieves me wood with much cunning'. By now they were within earshot of the guns, a sound 'not without a certain sublimity'. In command of a platoon, 2nd Lieutenant Wilfred Owen was also its servant, for his duty was to care for its needs and well-being; he wrote to Susan,

'...this very day I knelt down with a candle and watched each man perform his anointment with Whale Oil: praising the clean feet, but not reviling the unclean.'

Also in this letter, he assures her, 'I cannot do a better thing or be in a righter place.'

If Susan Owen was reassured by this confidence, she must have been shaken by the change in his tone less than week later. By now he was in the heart of the devastated landscape near Beaumont Hamel, scene of much heavy shelling and fierce fighting since the opening day of the Battle of the Somme six months earlier.

Visitors today find a quiet road running through a dip in the broad open uplands which are typical of the Somme landscape. In January 1917 this little valley was No Man's Land; as one

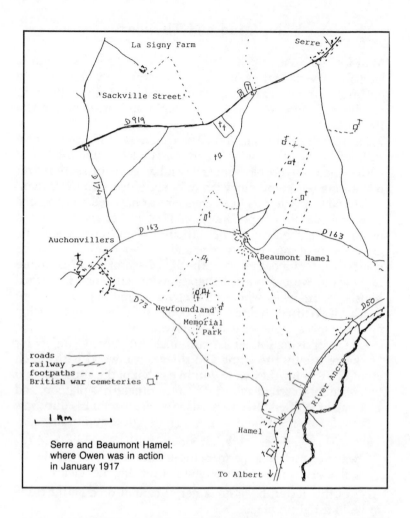

Famous villages and British cemeteries: the area where the 2nd Manchesters fought in 1917.

member of Wilfred's battalion described it in his diary, the 2nd Battalion approached the western ridge along three miles of shelled roads which were ankle deep in snow and mud and then marched for nearly three miles more along flooded trench and on down through La Signy farm (which still exists). Ahead was the smooth brow of hill held by the Germans with the steeper dip to the River Ancre beyond.

On 16 January Wilfred's usual carefully worked out presentation of incident and atmosphere slid into a detailed description of the fullest horror and misery in the exposed dangers of the front line. He was very straightforward about his distress:

> 'I can see no excuse for deceiving you about these last 4 days. I have suffered seventh hell. I have not been at the front. I have been in front of it. I held an advanced post, that is a 'dugout' in the middle of No Man's Land.'

He had been trapped below ground for more than two days by German shelling:

> 'My dug-out held 25 men tight packed. Water filled it to a depth of 1 or 2 feet, leaving say 4 feet of air. One entrance had been blown in and blocked. So far, the other remained. The Germans knew we were staying there and decided we shouldn't. Those fifty hours were the agony of my happy life. Every ten minutes on Sunday afternoon seemed an hour. I nearly broke down and let myself drown in the water that was now slowly rising over my knees.'

The long, tight-packed and shatteringly noisy hours of shelling as they crouched in the cramped dark concrete dug-out were a severe initiation for a new subaltern with a tendency to nightmares about suffocation. One of the sentries was blasted down the steps of the shelter by the explosions and blinded, an incident which inspired Wilfred's poem *The Sentry*, started several months after the experience and completed more than a year later:

> 'We'd found on old Boche dug-out, and he knew,
> And gave us hell; for shell on frantic shell
> Lit full on top, but never quite burst through.'

The events felt so deeply by 2nd Lt. Wilfred Owen and described so forcefully were not considered worth noting in his regiment's War Diary; and the precise location of the dug-out was not identified for over seventy years. Trench map references in surviving records and the knowledge that this was a German dug-out — and therefore with its entrances facing the German guns, making it even more dangerous to the newly-arrived British troops — have recently made it possible to locate the setting, in the No Man's Land of early 1917. Peaceful enough today, the

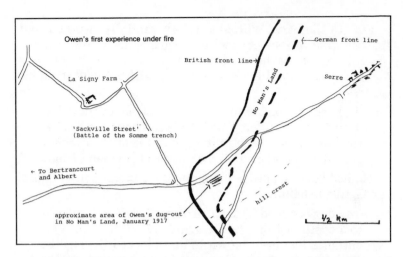

'The Sentry': trapped under bombardment, January 1917. The village of Serre, designated by the British as an objective for capture on the first day of the Battle of the Somme (1 July 1916), was still in German hands.

site of the dug-out lies between two British war cemeteries with their rows of headstones recording the murderous fighting there in 1916, 1917 and 1918 (see map page 22).

Early in February Wilfred was sent on a Transport Course in Abbeville. Perhaps this prompt departure from the front line indicates a lack of confidence in the new young officer: an attitude Wilfred himself may have realised, for his letter announcing his departure for a month, remarked that he would read his father's kind letters 'less shame-facedly in dug-outs and trenches than I do here in this pleasant peaceful town'. He was fortunate to be away from his battalion at this time; another Manchesters' man described in his diary what was supposed to be a 'rest period' out of the front line: 'Working parties during the day and guard at night. Hardest time of my life. About two hours' rest out of 24 every day'.

The severe cold continued and in Owen's hut his blanket was 'stiffish with frost' in the morning despite a petrol lamp kept alight beneath the bed. Meanwhile, the dangers of the front line remained at the back of his mind, ready to emerge later as poetry. Apart from the hours in the dug-out and the blinded sentry, there had been an encounter with gas (which eventually evolved into *Dulce et Decorum Est*) and further long hours endured lying out 'in the snow under the deadly wind' under close enemy scrutiny, when he marvelled that they did not all die of cold. The dull misery and dangers evoked so vividly in *Exposure* recreate this experience:

> 'Tonight, this frost will fasten on this mud and us,
> Shrivelling many hands, puckering foreheads crisp.
> The burying-party, picks and shovels in shaking grasp,
> Pause over half-known faces. All their eyes are ice,
> But nothing happens.'

Fellow officers were unaware of this poetic mind and instinct in their midst, and his eventual emergence as the voice of the oppressed would perhaps have surprised them. Meanwhile, a long-standing arrangement of writing poems on a topic agreed between himself, his cousin Leslie Gunston and their friend Olwen Joergens was still in operation and the course at Abbeville offered time for writing. In *Happiness*, begun during this period at Abbeville and revised six months later, he writes of the loss of youthfulness and childish pleasures: there is an awareness of himself as an adult looking back at the lost delights of boyhood:

> 'Boys' griefs are not so grievous as youth's yearning,
> Boys have no sadness sadder than our hope.'

British Encampment at Holnon, with smoke showing that these rough sheds were a warm refuge from the snow and mud. The Manchesters must have known this encampment so close to Savy Wood.

4. 'Such Intense Shelling'

Wilfred returned to his battalion at the end of February, travelling slowly. This was normal; throughout the war the whole area approaching and supporting the front lines was clogged with military transport and food supplies moving to and fro. Trains, lorries, buses and carts of all kinds were called into service, and individuals or small groups made their way as best they could. It took him a week to cover the 100 km from Abbeville to Bouchoir, travelling by stages through Amiens and on down the Roman road to the south-east.

Spring was in the air, and so was a change in the Western Front, for the Germans, unobserved by the British or French, had prepared a tactical withdrawal. The German armies had suffered as much as their allied opponents during the battles of 1916 and their generals had planned a new front line, the Hindenburg Line, which would be straighter and easier for them to reach, supply and defend. The new line ran closer to St. Quentin, some miles to the east of the Somme battlefield area, and by the time Owen rejoined his unit the Manchesters were moving forward through territory held by the invaders since the early days of the war.

Owen's active military life was interrupted by a disagreeable incident at Le Quesnoy-en-Santerre (near Bouchoir, 30 km from Amiens) when he fell into a cellar or shell-hole, on about 11 March 1917; apart from the fact that it happened in total darkness and that he was there for some twenty-four hours, little is known about this incident — Owen himself says that he felt nothing more than a headache for 3 days, before developing weakness, fever, pain and vomiting. He was out of action with concussion for about two weeks, evacuated first to Nesle military hospital and then to 13th Casualty Clearing Station at Gailly, on the River Somme.

Wilfred spent his time reading and drawing. He also drafted a sonnet for his brother Colin, *With an Identity Disc*, which was revised later in the year. (Lines from this poem form part of the memorial plaque set up in Ors in 1991.)

While 2nd Lieutenant Owen was travelling back to rejoin his battalion, it was moving forward under heavy fire through fields, woods and small villages to the west of St. Quentin. On April 1 they attacked towards the city and 'spent the night in a field bitterly cold and wet'.

Owen joined his men on April 2 near Savy, a few miles west of St. Quentin, just in time for an uninterrupted spell of four days of shelling 'without relief, in the open, and in the snow. (...) I kept alive on brandy, the fear of death and the glorious prospect of the cathedral Town just below us.' This was St. Quentin, unattainable behind its glittering rows of new barbed wire and defensive German positions.

The early signs of spring had vanished and the troops were surrounded by a quagmire of wet clay. While Owen was keeping watch as he lay out in the open, another member of the battalion describes how he 'lay down in 6" of mud and ice during a snowstorm' and had to dig in by the roadside 'wet through and feet frozen, can't get boots off to dry socks'. Blizzards added to their misery, in open country with little natural shelter.

Owen's letter recording these endurance tests also notes that a man crouching next to him has 'a beautiful round hole deep in his biceps' — an observation which perhaps inspired the unfinished poem *Beauty* written later in 1917 — while another, to Colin, was full of vigorous details of the kind appropriate for an admiring adolescent brother. He enclosed with it a bloodstained handkerchief taken from a crashed German Albatross scout plane — a souvenir more likely to appeal to Colin than to Susan. Both letters were written while the battalion was out of the front line, for a five day rest from 8 April.

Owen's next letter home bears the date 25 April, more than a fortnight later — a much longer interval than usual for this indefatigable correspondent. It had been an eventful period and he had much to report.

When they returned to the Savy area and their efforts to break through the Hindenburg Line, the battalion was instructed to support a French attack on 14 April. The designated assembly point, halfway between Fayet and the defensive lines on the north-west edge of St. Quentin, was not far away across the Roman road; but as they marched towards it, along trenches or over the open ground, they were met by artillery fire from St. Quentin. The battalion retraced its route and then swung round to the north past Selency and then past Fayet (which Owen was able to identify obliquely to his mother in a letter home), and along a small hollow known to the British as 'Squash Valley'. Getting to the assembly point from here meant crossing a bare hill-crest — and once more they were met with shell-fire: as Owen expressed it in writing home, 'Never before has the

Battalion encountered such intense shelling as rained on us as we advanced in the open'. Thirty of the Manchesters were killed here and Owen later used the experience in *Spring Offensive*:

'So, soon they topped the hill, and raced together
Over an open stretch of herb and heather
Exposed.'

The steady advance continued despite these losses and the Battalion earned high praise from their commanding officer, Colonel Luxmoore. Writing to Colin later, Wilfred described his impression of the advance:

'The sensations of going over the top are about as exhilarating as those dreams of falling over a precipice, when you see the rocks at the bottom surging up at you. I woke up without being squashed. Some didn't. There was an extraordinary exultation in the act of slowly walking forward, showing ourselves openly. (. . .) Then we were caught up in a Tornado of Shells. The various "waves" were all broken up and we carried on like a crowd moving off a cricket field. When I looked back and saw the ground all crawling and wormy with wounded bodies I felt no horror at all but only an immense exultation at having got through the Barrage.'

The vivid and disturbing images of his poem *The Show*, written six months later, recreate this image of the wounded men in the open field and reveal the intensity of the experience and its effect on the poet.

The battalion advanced past Cepy Farm[3] and attacked their objective, Dancour Trench; ironically, after the slaughter of the attack, they found it empty: '. . . fortunately there was no bayonet work, since the Hun ran before we got up to his trench'. As he wrote a little later,

'I rather enjoyed the evening after the Stunt, being only a few hundred yds from the Town, as you knew, and having come through the fire so miraculously: and being, moreover, well fed on the Bosche's untouched repast!! It was curious and troubling to pick up his letters where he had left off writing in the middle of a word!'

[3] Cepy Farm still exists. The area of this approach and attack can be seen clearly from the new bridge over the A26 motorway on the small road from Selency to Fayet.

Despite this success they were unable to rest, for '... we were kept up (in another part of the line) for 9 days after it: under incessant shelling'.

They were back in Savy Wood during this period, consolidating the main trench line close to the heavily fortified Hindenburg Line where it swelled forward round the western edges of St. Quentin. It was here in the wood that Owen's mental condition deteriorated. During one bombardment he was blown half-asleep into the air as he lay against a railway embankment; and in the following days, spent '... in a railway cutting, in a hole just big enough to lie', he felt that the dismembered body of his friend Lt. Hubert Gaukroger was near by. Owen wrote of his fellow officer that

> 'he was covered with earth, and no relief will ever relieve him, nor will his Rest be a 9-days rest. (...) it makes us feel bitterly towards those in England who might relieve us, and will not.'

Gaukroger, however, had never been in Savy Wood, either before or after his death: he was killed on April 2, as the Battalion

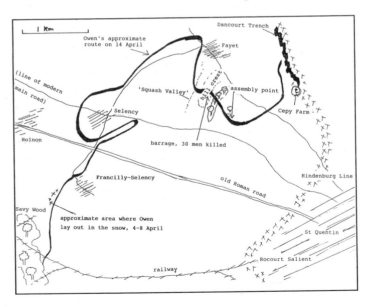

Into the attack — lying out in the open, 4—8 April, the route to the empty trench, and Savy Wood where Owen lay in a cramped hole in a railway cutting as his shell-shock was developing.

was moving up from the village of Savy, and is buried in Savy British war cemetery. Owen's mistaken belief that Gaukroger lay 'in various places around and about', as he rather tactlessly wrote to his sister Mary, may indicate the confusion of his mind after the days spent in the darkness of his solitary hole. It is not known whose shattered body shared his lonely hours there, although it may have been that of 2nd Lt. Harry Winch of the Army Cyclists Corps, who was attached to the 2nd Manchesters. The days spent concealed in Savy Wood clearly added yet another distressing experience to the fall and concussion in March and being pinned down by shell-fire in the flooded dug-out in January. It is impossible to know how the confusion developed in Owen's mind as the symptoms of shell-shock developed, both in the railway bank and afterwards: the literal darkness surrounding him on this occasion, as with the previous incidents, seems to match his mental state.

On April 21 the Battalion was relieved and moved back to Quivières for what was officially a rest period, but which entailed steady work all day — 'we rise at 6.15 and work without break until about *10 pm*'. On 1 May it was noticed that Owen's behaviour was not normal. The Battalion Medical Officer found him shaky, tremulous and confused in memory and he was dispatched to the 13th Casualty Clearing Station, which he had left only recently after recovering from concussion.

On that occasion he had been able to return to action after two weeks; now, although he assured his mother that he was not having a 'breakdown' but was avoiding one, he managed to admit to Susan that 'my nerves have not come out without a scratch', and was to have a much longer period away. After the war Owen's Commanding Officer was said to have remarked at the time that Owen was 'not fit to lead his men', a supposed accusation of cowardice which led to argument and distress among Owen's family and friends.

Victims of neurasthenia — the name given to Owen's nervous condition — were usually quick to recover; the Casualty Clearing Station's psychiatrist reckoned to discharge nearly three-quarters of his patients back to their units within three weeks. The pattern of Owen's treatment, requiring five months in one hospital or another and another nine months in training again before being judged fit for active service, is an indication of how deeply he was affected.

His first hospital, the Casualty Clearing Station at Gailly on the Somme, was a pleasant one. The river which gave its name to the surrounding *département* and to the costly battle of 1916 was almost invisible to the troops engaged in the fighting. It wound in leisurely fashion along a quiet valley, looping to and fro between willows and poplars — a haven for birds and fishermen in peacetime and for weary soldiers at war. (The French-held sector of the Somme valley nearer to Péronne, on the other hand, was the scene of long and bitter struggles at various stages of the war.)

Casualties were sometimes transported to Amiens by water and Owen's poem *Hospital Barge* was inspired by a journey along the canal which provides a straight and efficient shipping channel close to the river's meanderings; written at the end of 1917, it recalls a hot and sleepy afternoon which reminded Wilfred of his juvenile readings, of Avalon or the *Faerie Queen*:

> 'Budging the sluggard ripples of the Somme,
> A barge round old Cerisy slowly slewed.'

During this time of stress and illness the religious framework of Owen's childhood and education overcame his dislike of the Church as he had experienced it. As he wrote to his mother on May 16,

> 'I am more and more Christian as I walk the unchristian ways of Christendom. (. . .) one of Christ's essential commands was: Passivity at any price! Suffer dishonour and disgrace; but never resort to arms. Be bullied, be outraged, be killed; but do not kill.'

His mother, whose faith was one of endurance and passivity, must have appreciated this statement but may have wondered at its contrast with Wilfred's decision to enlist and to fight. Part of the essence of his attitude to war surfaced some months later in his poem *At a Calvary near the Ancre*.

In the middle of June Owen's name appeared on the list of officers to be evacuated to England. After ten days in Netley Hospital in Hampshire he was sent to Edinburgh and travelled via London in order to buy some clothes; and then, on June 26, 1917, he arrived at Craiglockhart War Hospital, on the outskirts of Edinburgh.

5. Craiglockhart

When Wilfred Owen walked up the broad steps of the tall, imposing and rather severe building[4] he can scarcely have imagined its future importance in his life. In later years Craiglockhart has become a lively university building — but in 1917 it was a former health resort hotel. Converted for use in restoring health of a different kind, its crowded bedrooms and grand reception rooms were full of officers overwhelmed by the intolerable experience of war. The lofty rooms and the long corridors are bright and cheerful now, but in 1917 their dark paint was a challenge to claustrophic shell-shocked men fresh from living half-underground in the trenches.

Owen arrived in Edinburgh by the overnight train from London, 'breakfasted hugely' at the station hotel and then walked 'the lovely length' of Princes Street. No doubt he recalled the family's Scottish holiday in 1912, which included a visit to Edinburgh, for he now found 'the Castle looked more than ever a Hallucination, with the morning sun behind it'.

He was to find more than enough hallucinations inside the hospital. By day the patients had occupation and companionship, but by night the hospital was haunted by nightmares and uncontrolled memories stalking the sleep of men who had seen, heard, smelt, endured too much, until their minds gave way. It was a period when 'shell-shock' and associated mental distress of various kinds were often not properly recognised and when men suffering from severe war-induced mental anguish might simply be accused of cowardice. Effective treatment developed slowly in response to the new forms of warfare.

Captain Brock,
Wilfred Owen's medical officer
at Craiglockhart.

[4]The building, in Colinton Road, is now the Craiglockhart site of Napier University. In his *Sherston's Progress*, Siegfried Sassoon describes the hospital under the name of Slateford.

Wilfred Owen was assigned to the care of Captain Arthur Brock of the Royal Army Medical Corps, who shared his interest in botany. The atmosphere created in the hospital by Brock and his colleague Captain W. H. R. Rivers (known to readers of Siegfried Sassoon's fictionalised *George Sherston* memoirs) was energetic and positive, based on a philosophy of bringing patients back to a civilised and natural relationship with the world around them. Disturbed patients should be healed through ordinary society and application to some outside activity relevant to their own interests and talents.

Wilfred was encouraged by Dr. Brock to revive his interest in botany by joining the Field Club and its long walks into the Pentland Hills close to Craiglockhart. His literary enthusiasm and talents were directed towards the hospital journal, *The Hydra*; he was soon its editor, and the days became pleasantly busy as he wrote editorials or prepared to address the Field Club.

Patients were encouraged to face the horrors which they had encountered, to acknowledge and thereby overcome them. Dr. Brock presented Wilfred with a singularly appropriate topic which was one of the doctor's own favourite themes — the ancient Greek legend of the giant who could not be defeated as long as he remained in touch with his mother the Earth. Antaeus, the giant, was overcome by Hercules, who held him off the ground until his strength had vanished. Owen, who had so recently had all too much contact with 'mother Earth' — and whose relationship with his own mother was all-important — must have realised the significance of a healthy relationship with the world around him. The legend appears in *The Wrestlers*, the unfinished poem drafted within his first two months at Craiglockhart. Dr. Brock discussed the significance of the legend in an article for *The Hydra*:

'Now surely every officer who comes to Craiglockhart recognises that, in a way, he is himself Antaeus who has been taken from his Mother Earth and well-nigh crushed to death by the war giant or military machine... Antaeus typifies the occupation cure at Craiglockhart. His story is the justification of our activities.'

In contrast to his youthful habit of referring frequently to his health when writing home, Owen's letters at this time are generally silent on his symptoms — although a letter in the middle of August commented that he had 'had some very

*Craiglockhart
in the 1990s.*

bellicose dreams of late'. A further possible cause for distress
at this time may have been the supposed accusation of
cowardice. This has never been fully defined or explained,
although Wilfred's new acquaintances in Edinburgh were aware
that he was much concerned about it.

Like other patients, Wilfred was sent out to explore Edinburgh,
to write papers on what would now be known as local history
and sociological topics, to visit sympathetic local families and
generally to be as active as possible. He soon acquired friends
locally and was popular in the school where he briefly did some
teaching. Family visits were encouraged and Wilfred did not feel
happy or settled until his mother had visited him in Edinburgh,
which she did towards the end of July.

In mid-August the course of his life — and the development
of twentieth century poetry — was changed by a new arrival in
Craiglockhart. As Wilfred hastened to announce to his cousin
Leslie Gunston, 'At last I have an event worth a letter. I have
beknown myself to Siegfried Sassoon'.

This would have been an important matter to any young poet
for, during the war, Sassoon — after several years of publishing

34

slim volumes of mild poetry — had made a name for himself as the writer of short, ferocious and incisive poems which brought home to civilians some of the savagery of the war; he was also famous in wider, non-literary circles, for a dramatic protest against what he saw as the unnecessary continuation of the war. Sassoon was sent to Dr. Rivers' care in Craiglockhart less because he was suffering from shell-shock — although his experiences on the Western Front had left him with hallucinations as well as the award of the Military Cross — than because he was an embarrassment to the authorities.

Sassoon's very public gesture could not be ignored. He was well-connected, admired and heroic, and he had deliberately thrown his Military Cross ribbon into the River Mersey; he hoped to be court-martialled to gain further publicity for his protest against the war. The suggestion of Sassoon's fellow Welch Fusilier, Robert Graves, that he should instead be sent to a 'hospital for mental disorders' was greeted with relief by the military hierarchy — and the conventional country gentleman who had turned into an unorthodox and dynamic poet now languished in Craiglockhart, unhappy and frustrated.

Sassoon's boredom in the establishment which he nicknamed 'Dottyville' was interrupted by Owen knocking at his door and shyly introducing himself, initially in order to seek his signature on copies of his recent book *The Old Huntsman*. This done, their conversation moved naturally to the writing of poetry; and before long the two men — ludicrously different in their appearance, with Sassoon a foot taller than Owen — fell into the habit of discussing and analysing each other's work.

Wilfred, in his usual way of hero-worshipping and building on the style of writers whom he admired, briefly took to writing poems in Sassoon's style — a very prompt reaction, for his letter to Leslie Gunston announcing his first visit to Sassoon's room also included a draft of *The Dead-Beat*, deliberately following Sassoon's direct and down-to-earth manner. Although scores — hundreds — of men and officers wrote 'war poetry', Sassoon's type of protest against the war was unique and it was Owen's good fortune to meet, at just the right moment, the man whose instincts and achievements he admired and who was prepared to offer him interest and support.

Their meeting and their many conversations were the catalyst he needed. From then on his writing was not only a healing exercise — working through the front-line experiences which had so undermined his stability — but also a direct expression of his powerful feelings of sympathy and compassion for suffering humanity.

He used Sassoon as a tutor, submitting work for criticism, and the older man, who wrote half ruefully to others about his new young friend's assiduous attentions, was generous with his time and attention. Wilfred's earlier literary friendship, with Laurent Tailhade in his Bordeaux days, resurfaced in his use of words and half-rhymes; and, while the great armies of Britain and Germany faced each other in the mud and endless slaughter of Passchendaele through the late summer and autumn of 1917, the two poets in Scotland spent their days in walking, playing golf (Sassoon), preparing *The Hydra* (Owen) and discussing poetry.

The events of the war now began to appear with growing power in Owen's writing, which had not until now dealt with the raw experiences of front line action. Specific incidents in action earlier that same year rose to the surface and spilt on to the page through many drafts — such as *Dulce et Decorum Est*, recalling Wilfred's first encounter with gas in January:

'— An ecstasy of fumbling,
Fitting the clumsy helmets just in time;
But someone still was yelling out and stumbling,
And flound'ring like a man in fire or lime...
Dim, through the misty panes and thick green light,
As under a green sea, I saw him drowning.'

His improving mental health and the friendship, interest and encouragement of a well-known poet increased his confidence and the poems written or drafted at this time show his rapidly growing maturity, while Sassoon for his part moved from a slightly patronising attitude to generous acknowledgement of a greater talent. The development of *Anthem for Doomed Youth* reflects their efforts, with Sassoon suggesting a couple of minor alterations which were retained in the final version of the poem. Dr. Brock's prescription of overcoming shell-shock by facing it and working through it was being carried out to the letter.

Time available after attending to *The Hydra* — either as editor or contributor — was further occupied with visits, German lessons and social life in Edinburgh. By early September Owen wrote to his mother that 'I still have disastrous dreams, but they are taking on a more civilian character, motor accidents and so

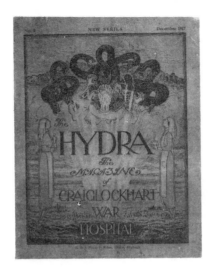

Cover of The Hydra, *December 1917, with three contributions by Sassoon. One of the advertisements in this issue (trench coats, military pattern boots, Christmas cards with regimental crests etc.) offers 'Books of Interest — including 'Gone West — After-death Experiences of three officers killed at the Front'.*

on.' This must have been a relief from more agonised moments; a cartoon in *The Hydra* shows typical nightmare scenes, with a startled man surrounded in his bed by swooping demons in gas masks.

Owen met another poet in October. This was Robert Graves, who came to visit his friend Sassoon. Graves took to Owen and was impressed by his writing, and the two more experienced and more highly educated men effectively became Wilfred Owen's literary godfathers.

Owen was now enjoying the heady experience of seeing his work in print — not only the editorial features in *The Hydra* but, in September 1917, his first printed poem — *Song of Songs*, in the same journal. Responding to Sassoon's advice to 'sweat your guts out writing poetry', he drafted and developed several other poems at this time. Some reveal Sassoon's influence (*Inspection*, for example), and others show his continuing interest in the technicalities of half rhyme. *From my Diary, July 1914*, which was probably drafted at this time, is concerned not with the trials of war but with memories of life in the Pyrenees in the summer of 1914. Luxuriating in the exercise of sounds and impressions, the poem shows Owen's imagination expanding and putting his growing maturity into practice.

Disabled on the other hand, which was drafted at Craiglockhart in October 1917, is an unsparing picture of life for some of the war's victims — the young man who is now mutilated in body and old in mind, his vigour spent: 'He's lost his colour very far from here'. It was Graves's response to this poem which stung Owen into a declaration of independence; he wrote later to Sassoon that 'It seems Graves was mightily impressed and considers me a kind of *Find*! No thanks Captain Graves! I'll find myself in due time.' And *Mental Cases*, written in the following spring, also depicts the casualties of war:

'— These are men whose minds the Dead have ravished.
Memory fingers in their hair of murders,
Multitudinous murders they once witnessed.'

Writing poetry which stemmed from intense personal experience, and learning how to write more effectively, was a major part of the cure for Owen's depression and nightmares. By late October he was passed fit to leave Craiglockhart, although not yet ready to return to active service.

Sassoon was distressed at the news; the two men spent a final evening together in an Edinburgh club where they shocked another diner with their vigorous amusement over some absurd and overwritten verses sent to Sassoon. As Sassoon recorded later, 'The more we laughed, the more solemnly he eyed us, and this somehow made our hilarity uncontrollable.' They must have been an odd and entertaining sight themselves, the two officers of such different appearance swept by gales of schoolboy laughter. As Owen left to catch the midnight train to London Sassoon pressed an envelope into Owen's hand; it proved to contain a £10 note and an address which would be useful to him in London.

6. 'The True Measure of Man'

The overnight train from Edinburgh took Wilfred Owen back into the outside world on 4 November 1917: he had exactly twelve months to live.

His first destination was Shrewsbury, to see his family and show them that he was fit and free from shell-shock; and the first letter written from home was to Siegfried Sassoon. More outspoken than his reserved friend, Owen acknowledged the warmth of his affection and the depth of his gratitude — Sassoon, he said, had 'fixed' his life. The note which Sassoon passed to Owen as they parted in Edinburgh included an introduction to Robert Ross, one of the leading literary figures of the day. This was a significant gesture, for more than one reason.

Ross was an art dealer, and a considerable patron and benefactor of young writers and artists; a man of wealth and style, he was generous to his many friends and made them welcome at his establishment in Mayfair. When he died, one obituary recorded that 'friendship was the chief business of his life', but to the world at large he was known principally as the intimate and long-standing friend and editor of Oscar Wilde. This connection continued to be of considerable significance in Ross's life, for after Wilde's trial and downfall he was inevitably involved in the surrounding accusations and ostracism. When Owen met him, memories of Wilde's notorious trial in 1895 had been revived by persistent persecution from Lord Alfred Douglas, Wilde's erstwhile lover; Ross, whose sexual and personal inclinations were in sympathy with Wilde's, had learned discretion — but his circle of friends included many homosexuals and the atmosphere of literary freedom and sexual tolerance was one of liberation for an aspiring poet from a modest provincial background.

All aspects of Owen's life now came together to his advantage; the shattering experiences of warfare had been faced and assimilated, his poetry had clearly found its true note and he was among educated and stimulating intellectual companions. Sassoon's gesture of introducing Owen to Ross — in the knowledge that Ross's approval would lead to further valuable introductions and friendships — indicated his acknowledgement of a kindred spirit. Owen came from a prudish and restricted background where sexual matters were never discussed and where writing poetry was a lonely occupation; in addition to releasing Wilfred's self-confidence and instincts for distinctive poetry, Sassoon enabled him to enter a world where he felt naturally and easily at home. This was where his true adult personality and talents would be recognised and accepted.

The group of writers, friends and literary acquaintances which Owen now joined was to be a broad one, ranging from the discreet circle of literary homosexuals such as Ross himself, Sassoon and Osbert Sitwell to well-known figures such as H. G. Wells and Arnold Bennett. Friendship with Ross led Owen to Oscar Wilde's writings, where he found much that pleased him and gave him added confidence.

After three weeks of this stimulating London life Owen was posted to Scarborough, the seaside resort on the Yorkshire coast which he had once visited on a family holiday. A reserve battalion of the Manchester Regiment was stationed in Burniston Barracks, but the Officers' Mess, to which Owen — on light duties — was appointed 'major-domo', was comfortably established in the imposing Clarence Gardens Hotel on the North Cliff (later renamed the Clifton and still in existence).

Controlling the household meant managing a team of cleaners, cooks, batmen, orderlies and gardeners, chasing round after them and urging them on. Owen had a room to himself which was very much to his liking — a turret bedroom with five windows looking out over the town and the sea, with an open fire to combat the cold winds off the North Sea. His chief concern, as he wrote to his mother towards the end of November, was that the Commanding Officer's bathwater should not be cold, nor his plates too hot; 'Life here is a mixture of wind, sand, crumbs on carpets, telephones, signatures, clean sheets, shortage of meat, and too many money-sums. But I like it.'

To his cousin Leslie Gunston he now expressed an idea which seems a long way from their juvenile experiments in writing poetry: 'I think every poem, and every figure óf speech should be a *matter of experience*.' He had of course accumulated a good deal of raw experience by now and was conscious that his cousin, for one reason or another, could not match this.

Owen had a busy winter. Quite apart from his housekeeping duties, his waking hours were concerned with the poems that were growing out of events of the past year — *Hospital Barge at Cerisy* from his second period in the Casualty Clearing Station, *Apologia pro Poemate Meo*, *The Show* — a disturbing

The Owen family without Wilfred: Susan and Tom, with from left to right, Harold, Colin and Mary.

echo of the events by Savy Wood in April — and others. *The Show* may owe something to the French account of trench warfare which was creating a stir at the time, Henri Barbusse's *Le Feu* (immediately translated into English, as *Under Fire*).

In January he attended Robert Graves's wedding to Nancy Nicholson and at the reception afterwards, as he proudly reported to his cousin, he was introduced to fellow guests as 'Mr. Owen, Poet', or 'Owen, the poet'. This followed a recent letter from Graves, remarking in his usual blunt way, 'Don't make any mistake, Owen, you are a damned fine poet already'. It was also a pleasing echo of his own end-of-year letter to his mother in which, reviewing the year as she had taught him to do, he commented that 'I go out of this year a Poet, my dear Mother, as which I did not enter it'.

The same letter expressed for the first time his view of his own future: he was thinking, he wrote, of the strange blind look he had seen on the faces of the men at the great training camp in Etaples when he first arrived in France twelve months earlier. 'To describe it', he wrote, 'I think I must go back and be with them'. The way ahead was clear, as both soldier and poet.

The second and even more significant event that month was the first national publication of a poem by Wilfred Owen — *Miners*, which appeared in the weekly journal *The Nation*. Initially inspired by a severe pit explosion earlier that month in which 140 miners died, the poem links the ancient history of the earth to coals burning peacefully in a grate (presumably the open coal fire in Wilfred's turret room in Scarborough) and to men and boys who die underground for the sake of comfortable fires in warm rooms. It evokes too the victims of war; mining skills were employed all along the Western Front and many men were trapped and killed below ground.

Wilfred Owen, the son of an assistant railway superintendent from Monkmoor Road, Shrewsbury, was accepted now by men whose publications and literary opinions he admired, in whose company he felt free — despite their many advantages of education, sophistication and wealth — and now he was a published poet! It is hardly surprising that he was not concerned to join in the social life of the Officers' Mess; games of bridge were not for him when he had his quiet room waiting for poetry to be written. His fellow officers dismissed him as uninteresting.

Owen was slowly getting closer to the war again; early in March a medical board upgraded him and he moved to the vast Northern Command depot at Ripon where he was billeted

in a dirty and disagreeable camp. However, soon after his twenty-fifth birthday (18 March 1918) he discovered a small cottage to let in Borrage Lane, on the edge of the town. It made a perfect lodging, a pleasant walk away from the camp, with the special bonus of a quiet attic room in which to work. Here he settled down after the day's military activities and applied his mind to poetry.

Taking his friend Sassoon's advice, Owen deliberately drew on the distress and terrors of front line experience and shell shock to

Ripon in the 1990s: the Borrage Lane cottage that Wilfred rented in March 1918.

write truthfully about the war. The intentional recollections summoned up nightmares once more, but he knew his theme and his craft did not waver. Writing, drafting, polishing with unremitting energy, he applied his hard won skills and shaped his poems from intense personal knowledge. *Futility* dates from this period, with its tenderness and despair, and, in *The Send-Off*, the quiet awareness of battles ahead:

'Shall they return to beating of great bells
In wild train-loads?
A few, a few, too few for drums and yells,
May creep back, silent, to village wells,
Up half-known roads.

Full of the deep feeling and shared experience which gave him the right to speak for the inarticulate soldier, his work now reveals the voice of a man who has seen far too much of war to tolerate 'drums and yells' as a proper response to battle.

At the same time the war was taking a new and alarming turn, for 1918 brought fresh threats to the British armies in France and Flanders. In mid-March — as Wilfred Owen celebrated his birthday with visits to Fountains Abbey and Ripon Cathedral — the Germans launched a powerful offensive which surged westwards across much of the ground so dearly contested in earlier fighting; the Allied armies suffered enormous losses in casualties as well as territory. Wilfred recognised that the terrain near St. Quentin where he had fought more than a year earlier was back in German hands and by late March the devastated slopes of the River Ancre were lost yet again. As Wilfred wrote bitterly to his sister, 'They are dying again at Beaumont Hamel, which already in 1916 was cobbled with skulls.'

Perhaps he realised that the desperate events in France would hasten his return to the front line, as casualties mounted and the army's needs increased.

In April 1918 there was leave, and time for a weekend at home. His brother Harold was there: in his memoirs he recounts how the two brothers were left together late in the evening to talk together. After some desultory conversation Harold remarked 'You have made up your mind to get back to the front line as soon as possible, haven't you?' 'Yes I have, Harold, and I know I shall be killed. But it's the only place that I can make my protest from.' They talked on about the war and fell asleep in front of the fire. Next day Harold accompanied Wilfred to the station; they were not to meet again.

On his next break from military routine he dined with Ross and met Osbert Sitwell and made another new friend in this attractive world of London literary men. Charles Scott Moncrieff, a writer, poet and outstanding translator who was one of Ross's homosexual friends, was strongly attracted to Owen. He worked at the War Office, where he did his best to have Owen posted as lecturer to a cadet battalion. By now, however, Wilfred had been upgraded once more, moving up the scale towards fitness for general active service; quiet postings in England were not easy to find and at a time of such desperate need of men to fight it seems unlikely that Owen could have avoided returning to France.

It is clear, indeed, from the tone of his letters and poems that he had come to a firm decision. His vocation now — so confusing and contradictory when he was at Dunsden and considering entering the Church — was to be with the ordinary soldiers, to lead them and to speak for them. He must prove his own worth and proclaim the true nature of war; civilians in England must be made to understand what was being endured in their name.

The world of poetry laid claim to Owen once more when the Sitwells sent an urgent request for his poems for their 1918 anthology *Wheels*. (In due course they dedicated the 1919 volume of *Wheels* to Owen and included in it *Strange Meeting, The Show, A Terre, The Sentry, Disabled, The Dead-Beat* and *The Chances*.) Meanwhile, on June 18 *The Nation* published *Hospital Barge at Cerisy* and *Futility*. As he remarked to his mother at the end of May, such success would have turned his head five years ago — but now 'I want no limelight and celebrity is the last infirmity I desire. *Fame is the recognition of one's peers.*'

In July Osbert Sitwell, who clearly regarded Owen as 'his peer', wrote to him with an epigram on Clemenceau, the French Premier, which used religious phrasing to sharpen its irony. Owen's response included a paragraph on his own army life, full of echoes of Sitwell's lines and of Wilfred's own religious upbringing and his struggle with his faith:

'For 14 hours yesterday I was at work — teaching Christ to lift his cross by numbers, and how to adjust his crown; and not to imagine he thirst till after the last halt; I attended his Supper to see that there were no complaints; and inspected his feet to see that they should be worthy of the nails. I see to it that he is dumb and stands to attention before his accusers. With a piece of silver I buy him every day, and with maps I make him familiar with the topography of Golgotha.'

Owen himself was already all too familiar with that modern Golgotha.

The letter was written in July 1918, the time of what turned out to be the final German advance. Paris was under threat, as it had been in the distant summer of 1914 — but the German troops had reached the furthest point of their advance west. The vital road and rail junction of Amiens had had a narrow escape in March but the United States Army was making its presence felt and now, on the Marne, the balance between the weary armies was shifting for the last time. From mid-July onwards, the conflict moved east and north as men everywhere — young, old, convalescent, half-fit — were called up to fill the ranks.

Two months earlier Wilfred had begun to assemble poems for a book with the intended title *Disabled & Other Poems*. The preface he was planning for this volume — which survives only as a rough draft but which is now as familiar as many of his most carefully revised and frequently quoted poems — states his philosophy without equivocation; and *The Calls*, written at about the same time, also makes a clear statement in its final stanza, expressing the soldier-poet's mood in those months of national anxiety and strain:

'I heard the sighs of men, that have no skill
To speak of their distress, no, nor the will!
    A voice I know. And this time I must go.'

The men who were fighting needed him to speak for them; and now he was fit for active service once more. On August 10 he had a medical inspection which passed him fit for draft. 'I am glad. That is I am much gladder to be going out again than afraid. I shall be better able to cry my outcry, playing my part.'

Embarkation leave enabled him to see Siegfried Sassoon again — having been wounded in the head, Sassoon was in hospital in London and knew that he would not be fit to return to the war again. On the last day of August Owen landed in France once more, over a year since his return to England in 1917 with shell-shock.

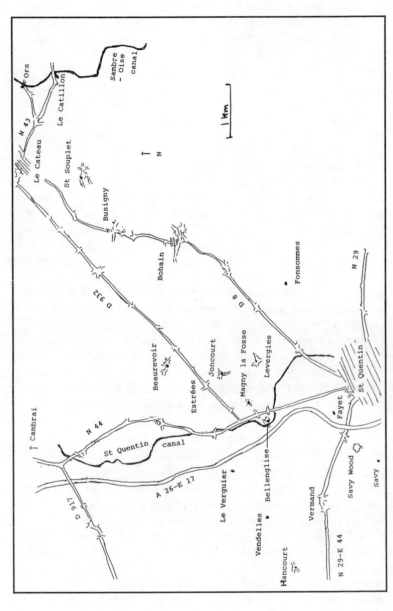

*The Route to Ors, September—November 1918,
showing modern main roads.*

7. Advancing, Attacking

Wilfred landed in France with recent memories of his mother and of Colin, his youngest brother, fresh in his mind. Colin, now a cadet in the Royal Air Force, was based in Hastings and Susan was able to visit her eldest and her youngest sons there before Wilfred's departure.

Owen spent a week in Etaples, the training camp near Boulogne. Letters were sent off to his mother and to Sassoon and there was time for poetry too: *The Sentry* (reviving his earliest front line experiences in 1917) and *Smile, Smile, Smile,* which showed the soldier's scorn for the safe complacent attitudes of civilians in England:

> ' — the half-limbed readers did not chafe
> But smiled at one another curiously
> Like secret men who know their secret safe
> (This is the thing they know and never speak,
> That England one by one had fled to France,
> Not many elsewhere now, save under France.)'

And *Spring Offensive,* begun at Scarborough earlier in the summer, recalls an incident of the Owens' childhood when he observed Harold's boots covered with buttercups — 'blessed with gold' — but now transferring the flower-gold to the 'slow boots' of the soldiers marching up towards the top of 'a last hill'.[5]

On September 13 Owen joined his battalion at Corbie, a few miles from Amiens. It had been involved in heavy fighting during August close to the Roman road between Amiens and St. Quentin when the German advance had pushed as far west as Villers Bretonneux, barely a dozen miles short of Amiens. The summer had been one of movement and alarm for the whole army as the pattern of static trench warfare broke up under the onslaught of the German advance. The British army was on the attack now, as the Germans, exhausted by the ferocity and initial success of their strategy, were pushed back towards their own frontiers, and the war moved into what was to become known as 'the last hundred days'. In late September, when Owen's battalion rejoined the British Fourth Army at Vendelles, the line had been driven back eastward once more, some 30 miles nearer to St. Quentin.

[5] It has also been suggested that this vivid image refers to the holiday in Broxton when Owen was 9 or 10, which included walks on the beautiful steep hillside.

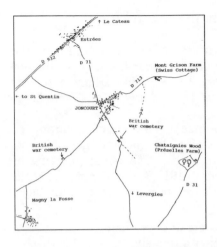

*Joncourt. On 1 October 1918
the Manchesters attacked the
final defence system of the
Hindenburg Line along the
ridge through Mont Grison
Farm and Chataignies Wood
(see maps, pages 50, 51 and 52).*

For twenty-four hours, beginning on 28 September 1918, the
gunfire thundering down on the Hindenburg Line was the
heaviest of any day throughout the whole war. Despite the Allied
advances there could be no relaxation, for up to the very end
of the war the mobile line was extremely dangerous and the
battle of the final advance cost the lives of 80,000 British troops.

Owen joined D Company, officially assigned as Bombing
Officer to the battalion despite his lack of specialised knowledge.
It must have seemed a curious quirk of fate to the Manchesters
that they were back near the area which they had fought over
so fiercely nearly 18 months ago; they were close to the section
of the Hindenburg Line where the events of April 1917 had led
to Owen's shell-shock.

His letters home during September 1918 are confident and
relaxed; he was clearly content to be back with the real war again
after the tedium of barracks life and training. He liked the other
officers in his Company, although he found the Battalion's
second in command somewhat less congenial. In a letter to his
mother at the end of September Wilfred described Major
Marshall of the Irish Guards, an alarming and much-wounded
winner of the Military Cross, as

'the most arrant utterly soldierly soldier I ever came
across. (. . .) Bold, robust, dashing, unscrupulous, cruel,
jovial, immoral, vast-chested, handsome-headed, of free,
coarse speech. . . '

Other officers, who seemed less daunting, referred to Wilfred

48

as The Ghost — perhaps because they had thought him dead at one point. Knowing nothing of his poetry-writing they regarded him as simply another officer returning to help in the Battalion's immense efforts.

Wilfred's next letter home, nearly a week later, was excited and triumphant, full of elation and the drama of being in action again. From Vendelles the Battalion had moved forward through Le Verguier towards the next German line of defence where the St. Quentin canal formed part of the Hindenburg Line. It was a strong defensive position, but it had been crossed successfully near Bellenglise. The main Hindenburg Line was backed by a support system and then a Reserve System, the whole sequence of strong lines covering a belt about four miles deep. The remains of the front line fortifications, strong-points and supply tunnels were visible to the Manchesters as they marched forward from their own reserve position.

As they approached the front line there were casualties close to Magny-la-Fosse, a village tucked almost invisibly into the folds of hill. The Manchesters and the units with them prepared to attack the strongly held Beaurevoir-Fonsomme section of the Hindenburg Reserve Line.

Moving uphill out of Magny-la-Fosse, the Manchesters advanced into action on 1 October. The brigade's first objective, the village of Joncourt, was taken without too much difficulty, but the next obstacle — which was allocated to the Manchesters — was the heavily wired and strongly held reserve line itself, the Germans' final fixed position.

The section facing the Manchesters ran along a smooth ridge to the east of the village, where remains of the concrete fortifications are still visible along the open hilltop. Joncourt has grown little since 1918 and it is still possible to stand by the church and look across the dip and sweeping rise of the opposite hillside. The modern visitor can see what Wilfred Owen and his men saw in 1918: the crest held by the Germans between the farm known to the British troops as Swiss Cottage, visible half a mile away to the left, and the tree tops of Chataignies Wood just appearing over the hilltop, further off to the right (see maps pages 50 and 51).

This was different from the churned-up hillsides of January 1917 and the maze of trenches in the woods and villages round St. Quentin where Wilfred Owen had last been in action. His

49

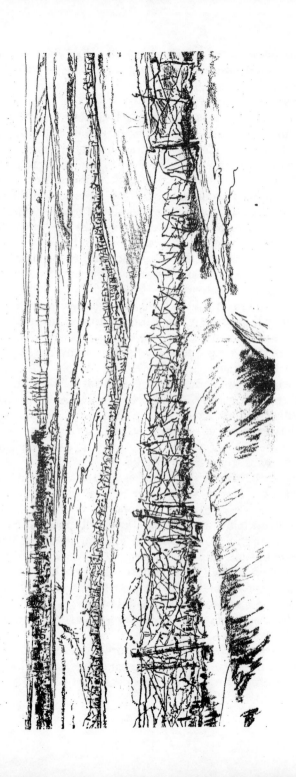

The Attacking Soldier's View, 1: the Beaurevoir—Fonsomme Line.

experiences then had overwhelmed his mind — but now his health and abilities as soldier and as poet were restored and ready.

Owen and his men were in the lead as the Manchesters attacked the strong line of German wire and machine-guns. They swept the defending troops back along their line from Swiss Cottage to Chataignies Wood, fifteen hundred yards to the south, and so far outstripped their companions that they found themselves isolated from the rest of the Battalion, in possession of a German machine-gun post and surrounded on three sides by enemy forces. 2nd Lt. Owen, now without a senior officer, took prisoners and turned the machine-gun on its original owners.

It was impossible to reach the wounded, to move further forward, or to withdraw; beleaguered, they had to remain there. As he wrote later to his mother:

> 'All one day (after the battle) we could not move from a small trench, though hour by hour the wounded were groaning just outside. Three stretcher-bearers who got up were hit, one after one. I had to order no one to show himself after that, but remembering my own duty, . . . I scrambled out myself and felt an exhilaration in baffling the Machine Guns by quick bounds from cover to cover.'

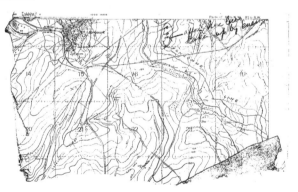

The Attacking Soldier's View, 2: a map preserved by the Manchester Regiment, showing the lines of wire near the top of the ridge and a pencilled ring indicating the approximate position being taken up by the enemy. British signalling stations are marked at the edge of Joncourt. The black dot to the right of 'C.C.S.' (for Casualty Clearing Station) in the village marks the church, from where there is a good view of the battle area.

The enemy line had been broken and the advance could continue; Wilfred Owen was immediately recommended for the Military Cross for his effective leadership and capture of the German machine gun. Lt. Foulkes, the subaltern with Owen during the attack who later recorded his memories of him, was quoted by Edmund Blunden in his lengthy 1931 memoir on Owen: 'Owen and I were the only officers left in our Company . . . This is where I admired his work — in leading his remnants, in the middle of the night, back to safety . . . I was content to follow him with the utmost confidence in his leadership.' This was scarcely the time for poetry, yet the intensity of concern which characterises Owen's affection for the ordinary soldiers at war — and which he expressed so fully in the best of his poems inspired by the war — is evident in his reactions to the incidents of battle. Early in the attack his soldier servant, Jones, was hit in the head, and fell across Owen so that the two men lay with the wounded man's blood soaking into Owen's shoulder. He wrote about it later to Sassoon:

> 'Catalogue? Photograph? Can you photograph the crimson-hot iron as it cools from the smelting? That is what Jones's blood looked like, and felt like. My senses are charred.'

The intensity of the struggle and the number of casualties — and his own success — were indicated obliquely:

> 'You will guess what has happened when I say I am now Commanding the Company, and in the line had a boy lance-corporal as my Sergeant-Major. With this corporal who stuck to me and shadowed me like your prayers I captured a German Machine Gun and scores of prisoners. I'll tell you exactly how another time. I only shot one man with my revolver (at about 30 yards!); the rest I took with a smile.'

Their advance and attack was one of the most successful elements of the day; Owen's Company, with one other, advanced further forward than any other troops that day — indeed they were the only Allied troops to reach the final line of the German system and, as surviving messages make clear, they were hard pressed to hold their position. A note from the Company's commanding officer has survived from that afternoon of the attack:

'All objectives gained Swiss Cottage is now ours 13 prisoners taken there C. Coy. getting into touch on right. There is no one up on our left. Enemy withdrawn. Full report follows'

The Battalion's commanding officer thanked all the men for their 'extremely gallant conduct' and noted that 'They are the only men in the Division who did their task and held it'. Outnumbered, they were threatened by German reinforcements; a terse note from the battlefield to the Manchesters' commanding officer, at 3.55 am on 2 October — twelve hours after their attack — states:

'The enemy are shoving forward on us. I am afraid of strong attack at dawn. May I have strong reinforcements at once. We have no one behind us.'

Owen and his men had to wait until darkness fell on the second night, 2 October, before the remains of the Company under their new temporary commanding officer could retreat safely.

To both Sassoon and his mother he described the act of fighting: this was the first time he had been in action since Savy Wood eighteen months earlier, with its distressing aftermath of shell-shock and the long months of treatment and recovery. Now, he wrote to his mother,

'I can find no word to qualify my experiences except the word SHEER. It passed the limits of my Abhorrence. I lost all my earthly faculties and fought like an angel.'

He used the same word, sheer, in his account to Sassoon, adding, 'I cannot say I suffered anything... my nerves are in perfect order.' Another comment to Sassoon reveals more of his own feelings about the war:

'I'm glad I've been recommended for M.C., and hope I get it, for the confidence it may give me at home. Full of confidence after having taken a few machine guns (with the help of one seraphic lance corporal,) I held a most glorious brief peace talk in a pill box.'

The battalion had suffered heavy losses and in his next letter home Owen explained one of his tasks: 'Must now write to hosts of parents of Missing, etc.' — but it was to Sassoon, his admired companion in military, literary and personal matters, that he confessed, 'I shall feel again as soon as I dare, but now I must not. I don't take the cigarette out of my mouth when I write

The War passes through. The village of Bohain in 1918, after the German retreat and the British advance. The Manchesters marched through Bohain to the front line in mid-October.

Deceased over their letters.' He had led his men back to safety, they had followed his confidence. Although Owen was no longer alive when the award of the Military Cross was announced, the citation confirmed that he had indeed 'played his part':

> 'For conspicuous gallantry and devotion to duty in the attack on the Fonsomme Line on 1st/2nd October 1918. On the Company Commander becoming a Casualty, he assumed command and showed fine leadership and resisted a heavy counter-attack. He personally manipulated a captured enemy machine gun in an isolated position and inflicted considerable losses on the enemy. Throughout he behaved most gallantly.'

Any lingering doubts about his fitness to lead his men had been thoroughly and publicly dispelled.

8. The Canal: November 1918

After this intensive period in action the Battalion was relieved on 3 October. They moved first slightly nearer to St. Quentin, and then two days later to Hancourt, halfway back to Péronne. The soldiers rested and Owen reflected. There was time now to assess his achievements in the battle: it was from here that he wrote the letters to his mother and to Sassoon describing the battalion's engagement and his own part in the day's achievements.

Sad news reached him here from Scott Moncrieff, of the deaths of two good friends — Robert Ross, who had died in London, and a war casualty, Philip Brainbrigge, a master at Shrewsbury School whom Owen had met while in Scarborough. He commented of the former that 'Robbie Ross's death is more affecting to me, almost, than many of the deaths that took place at my side'. Ross had been a valuable friend. Bainbrigge, a classicist of wit, short-sighted, and who wrote of himself at war as 'bored and afraid, irresolute and wet', was later described as 'unfit to fight in everything except courage'. Owen had dined with Bainbrigge in Shrewsbury, where he was virtually Wilfred's only link with the public school so close to his own home. The loss of two such gifted men from his growing circle of new friends would be felt after the war — and he knew that the war must end soon despite orders that 'Peace Talk must cease'.

Then on 18 October it was time for the Manchesters to move forward once more. The course of the war was progressing rapidly, and they marched across the terrain of their recent fierce encounter, past the villages of Bohain and Busigny, to rejoin the Line at St. Souplet on 22 October a few miles south of Le Cateau.

The line between the advancing British and the retreating Germans continued to shift north and east: by the end of October the Battalion was close to the Sambre-Oise canal east of Le Cateau and preparing to attack across the canal itself. Owen was anxious to reassure his mother about his own safety:

'We move from here in a few hours, *not* for the front. . . the roads are increasingly baffling; and though my letters cease for a week or more you *must not conclude I am in the fighting zone.*'

To his cousin Leslie Gunston, on the other hand, he stressed that 'You must not imagine when you hear we are 'resting' that we lie in bed smoking. We work or are on duty *always*'.

Despite Wilfred's assurances to Susan, the Manchesters were indeed close to the Germans and the front line. The next task, to cross the Sambre-Oise canal at Ors, was part of a larger scale onslaught coordinated between several units and designed to take the advancing British army across an awkward obstacle. The canal ran — as it still does — through low-lying ground, raised several feet above it along some stretches, with drainage ditches or reservoir pools along the side: so that the attacking British were faced with negotiating first the wet fields and then the bank of the canal. The rising ground on the opposite bank was strongly held, with German machine guns covering the canal itself.

The 96th Infantry Brigade, which included the 2nd Manchesters, took over the line west of the canal during the night of October 30-31. There were a few days in hand before attacking the canal — and plenty for the British troops to do in that time. Although the immediate approach to Ors and the canal consisted of small fields and orchards, a large wood covered much of the ground stretching back to Pommereuil, the nearest village, and down to the canal in places. This part of France had been occupied by the Germans throughout the war and this was the first time it had been fought over; there were no trenches or pill-boxes here, only scattered shell holes among the houses and orchards.

For their first two nights in the area, the battalion was fully occupied in reconnoitring and patrolling its 'patch', while their brigade neighbours, men of the 15th and 16th Lancashire Fusiliers, did the same in their area to the left. Between them they covered the west bank of the canal as far as the small town of Landrecies to the north, while from the right of the Manchesters' area, close to the village of Ors, men of the 1st Dorsets were responsible for the stretch of canal to the south.

The battalion had instructions to clear out any enemy presence west of the canal; some alarm posts were discovered and cleared on the night of 1-2 November. By the evening of 2 November, as the battalion diary notes briefly, 'the last enemy post was raided at dusk and exterminated. The only persons remaining alive were four who were taken prisoner, three Machine Guns along with them.'

The system was operating efficiently and morale was high —

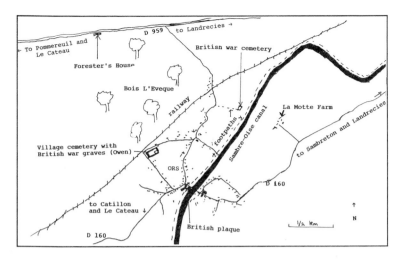

Modern Ors. The canal is best approached on foot: there is ample parking space in the village centre.

and as usual Wilfred found time to write cheerfully to his mother. On 31 October, the night his battalion arrived in the Ors area, he settled down in what he described as 'The Smoky Cellar of the Forester's House'.

'. . . So thick is the smoke in this cellar that I can hardly see by a candle 12 ins. away, and so thick are the inmates that I can hardly write for pokes, nudges and jolts. On my left the Coy. Commander snores on a bench: other officers repose on wire beds behind me. At my right hand, Kellett, a delightful servant of A. coy. in *The Old Days* radiates joy and contentment from pink cheeks and baby eyes. He laughs with a signaller, to whose left ear is glued the Receiver; but whose eyes rolling with gaiety show that he is listening with his right ear to a merry corporal, who appears at this distance away (some three feet) nothing but a gleam of white teeth and a wheeze of jokes.

'Splashing my hand, an old soldier with a walrus moustache peels and drops potatoes into the pot. By him, Keyes, my cook, chops wood; another feeds the smoke with the damp wood.

'It is a great life. I am more oblivious than alas! yourself, dear mother, of the ghastly glimmering of the guns outside, and the hollow crashing of the shells.

'There is no danger here, or if any, it will be well over before you read these lines.

'I hope you are as warm as I am; as serene in your room as I am here; and that you think of me never in bed as resignedly as I think of you always in bed. Of this I am certain you could not be visited by a band of friends half so fine as surround me here.'

Many miles back to the west of Ors, the trenches and shell holes near Beaumont Hamel have long been filled in and the embankment of the now disused railway line close to Savy Wood is barely visible, but Ors and its canal have changed little. There is still a Forester's House in the woodland outside Ors, in the 2nd Manchesters' area before the assault (see map, page 57). It is not difficult to imagine the plain brick cellar full of smoke and military companionship. Crowded amongst his men as he wrote to his mother, Wilfred could not guess the poignant significance of that final sentence.

The battle at Ors, 4 November 1918. This military map shows the positions of C and D Companies on the canal bank, dominated by la Motte Farm opposite, whilst the day's first and second objectives ('Yellow') and ('Blue') are just visible in the lower centre and bottom right sections.

November 3, the day before the attack, passed without incident. Enemy patrols on the east bank were noted, and the British troops kept up their own patrolling. Everyone went through repeated briefings, with orders for dealing with emergencies, and each officer's role was clearly defined.

The battalion attack was to take place with two Companies in the line (one led by Wilfred Owen), one in support and one in reserve. The canal was to be bridged by Royal Engineers after the initial five minutes' barrage directed on to the East bank of the canal; after crossing, the companies would re-form on the far side before advancing, with the artillery barrage advancing ahead of them, to their immediate objective, the slight rise and La Motte Farm a few hundred yards beyond the canal.

The Germans' natural advantages in this setting were obvious. Colonel Marshall (the redoubtable Major, now promoted, described earlier by Wilfred) voiced queries which were later quoted by Owen's fellow subaltern Potts. Marshall pointed out that on his own Battalion front (which lay next to that of the Manchesters), it was virtually impossible for the attack to succeed because the troops had first to cross the canal and then climb the slope which was heavily occupied with machine gun positions. The senior staff officer's response that 'the weight of the artillery from behind would blot out all opposition' was an ominous echo of promises made two years earlier; the heavy barrage before the Battle of the Somme was supposed to have eliminated all the enemy wire, but failed almost completely. Many of the casualties on 1 July 1916 were caused by the troops' inability to get through the German wire defences.

By this time the German armies had not only lost vast areas of ground which they had held throughout the war — in the last two months they had also lost 100,000 men captured by the Allies, while morale at home was so low that all hope of winning the war had vanished. But here beside the Sambre canal, as the Manchesters' battalion diary noted laconically, 'The enemy intended to hold this line to the bitter end' — while the British units in turn received specific orders that 'There is to be no retirement under any circumstances'.

Patrolling continued through the night of November 3, and by zero hour — 5.43 a.m. — on November 4 the battalion was ready, formed up on the edge of the village. It was an intensely dark night, with rain until midnight and then mist. In the grey half-light as dawn approached, the Manchesters waited through

Tranquillity Again. The canal, one kilometre north of Ors, in 1992.

the initial five-minute barrage; then as the barrage lifted and the whistles sounded they and the Royal Engineers rushed forward down the narrow lane and across the fields. The leading companies carried light bridges for crossing the ditches before they could reach the canal bank and provide covering fire.

The move was well-practised and carried out swiftly — but as the English artillery barrage lifted and directed its aim at the top of the rise beyond the canal, it was clear that it had not eliminated the German machine guns on the facing slope. Firing across the canal bank from beneath the new range of the British artillery, they aimed their machine guns at the bridge-building engineers and the protecting infantry units.

The British troops responded with equal vigour: attackers and defenders swept each other's lines with intense fire across the narrow gap. At the water's edge between them, the Royal Engineers brought up their special bridging units.

Men fell in the steady fire from the German guns, and the bridge splintered, but the British engineers worked until only two sappers were left. It was at this moment that the 19-year old James Kirk, a subaltern in the Manchesters, paddled himself and a machine gun out across the canal at the bullet-ridden heart of the struggle, firing his Lewis gun into the bristling array of enemy machine guns only a few yards away. The Germans were forced to take cover — which enabled two of the Royal Engineers

(Major Waters and Sapper Archibald) to finish mending the bridge. Kirk, wounded in the arm and the face, kept up his onslaught until he ran out of ammunition: more magazines were paddled out to him, he carried on firing again, and under this continuous cover the bridge was pushed out across the canal. Despite the smoke and tumult of battle in the surrounding semi-darkness, the whole construction of wooden floats linked with wire had been assembled in the record time of 30 minutes.

Built with such rapid skill and care, the bridge was hit again by shell-fire and damaged beyond repair. At the same instant James Kirk was wounded once more — this time fatally, shot through the head.

The swift work of the Royal Engineers and the Manchesters was repeated along the canal bank. The troops to their left succeeded in getting their bridge across the canal — but their commanding officer, Colonel Marshall, survivor of ten wounds earlier in the war, was killed as he was crossing the canal and they too were unable to continue. Marshall's fears over the inadequacy of the preliminary barrage had been proved well founded. As his adjutant recorded later, 'The upshot of it was complete failure. Marshall was killed trying to cross on the duckboards floating on petrol tins, and we had probably 100 casualties without moving an inch.'

And what about Wilfred Owen, in this confusion of noise and danger? As the Royal Engineers' bridge suffered under the shelling the Manchesters joined in the frantic efforts to repair the damage, then took to the rafts. It was still barely dawn and the battle was raging furiously in the mist, gas and darkness, the noise and withering fire. Owen's final movements remain unknown, part of that indescribable mixture of confusion and precision of fast-moving battle. Survivors later recorded his calm encouragement and support at the water's edge and it was reported afterwards that he had been hit and killed out on the water, on one of the rafts.

By the time it was fully light it was clear that no crossing could be made at this point and in text book fashion the units were withdrawn. Runners reported that their neighbouring unit, the Dorsets, had successfully bridged the canal just south of the village of Ors: the survivors of the Manchesters and the 16th Lancashire Fusiliers withdrew in good order and crossed there too. By midday the first objective, the low rise east of the canal, was in British hands. The 2nd Manchesters' official battalion diary reports the action:

'The attempt to bridge the Canal was under most terrific Machine Gun fire, heavy Trench Mortar Fire, and spasmodic artillery fire. The R.E.'s in throwing over the bridge worked in a magnificently gallant manner, but were decimated with perishing fire. An enemy shell knocked the bridge away and no further crossing of troops was possible. Repeated endeavours were made to get across but the fire from the opposite bank was intensely destructive.'

Four Victoria Crosses were awarded for that morning's work — to Second Lieutenant Kirk of the 2nd Manchesters, to Acting Lt.-Colonel Marshall, commanding officer of the Lancashire Fusiliers next to the Manchesters on the canal, and to Major Waters and Sapper Archibald of the Royal Engineers, both of whom survived. Kirk and Marshall are buried in the British corner of Ors village cemetery, in the same row as Lt. W. E. S. Owen, M.C.

A week after the set-back north of Ors and the successful crossing south of the village, the 2nd Manchesters greeted the Armistice at Sambreton, a few miles beyond the canal. As they laid down their arms and as the church bells were ringing throughout England to celebrate the end of the Great War on that morning of 11 November 1918, a more modest bell rang at the front door of the Owens' house in Shrewsbury. With awful irony it was at that precise moment that Susan and Tom Owen learned of Wilfred's death a week earlier.

The Memorial in Ors: presented by the Western Front Association and unveiled by the Chairman of the Wilfred Owen Association in 1991, in a ceremony organised by the Mayor and inhabitants of Ors.

9. The Beginning

The war was over and millions of men were dead, missing or mutilated in mind or body. The Spanish Flu epidemic had swept across the world. Who grieved for Wilfred Owen's death, and how widely was it noticed, this minor event in a world celebrating the end of the war? Where millions had mourned the death of Rupert Brooke in 1915, the loss of one more junior officer late in 1918 was surely of little consequence beyond his immediate family and his battalion.

Harold, on board his ship off the coast of South Africa when the war ended, learned of his family's loss in a curious way; he saw Wilfred in his cabin for a few moments — in a vision which soon vanished and left him, as he describes in his memoirs, with the certainty that Wilfred was dead.

Tom and Susan Owen saw Harold and Colin return safely from the war. The family continued to live in the same house in Shrewsbury for many years after the war and Mary, the quiet dutiful daughter, remained with her parents. For the headstone on her son's grave in the British war cemetery inside the village cemetery in Ors, a few hundred yards from the canal where he was killed, Susan Owen chose a quotation from one of his poems, *The End*, written over a long period and finished some time during the winter of 1917-1918:

'Shall Life renew these bodies? Of a truth,
All death will he annul'

What Wilfred actually wrote in the second of these lines was 'All death will he annul, all tears assuage?', followed by a despairing negative response, a denial of any hope for future salvation; Susan's choice of phrases and her omission of the second question-mark reverses her son's meaning and offers the visitor a devout but misleading interpretation.

In another respect, however, she followed Wilfred's intentions faithfully, by burning a large quantity of his papers unread — much against her will for, as she admitted to Sassoon, 'it was like burning my heart'; but she kept all his letters and well over six hundred survived. This copious mass of communication from Wilfred to his mother (although sadly none from Susan to him) is intensely revealing of Wilfred as a child, a loving and dutiful son, and as a maturing young man and developing poet.

We have no record of how most of Owen's London friends

reacted to his death, although Sassoon records that after the Armistice he waited to hear from him:

> 'Several months elapsed before I was told about his death. I have never been able to accept that disappearance philosophically. A blank miserable sense of deprivation has dulled my mind whenever I have thought of him... the chasm in my private existence remained.'

At the time of Wilfred's death his work was known only to his family — in effect his mother and his cousin Leslie Gunston — and a small London-based group of literary friends, remote from the Owens' quiet life in Shrewsbury. At one time Wilfred Owen was proud to think of himself as a Georgian poet — at least, that is what he wrote to his mother at the end of 1917 and to Leslie Gunston in January 1918. Later generations, however, have come to see Owen as a bridge between the traditions in which he grew up and those which followed the Great War, when the Georgian poets gave way to the various modern movements.

Since his death Owen's reputation has been like a slow-burning fuse, glowing steadily brigher through the decades. The various editions of Owen's work have brought considerable argument, for the many undated drafts of a poem have made accurate dating, and therefore the poet's final intentions, extremely difficult.

The 1919 edition of the Sitwells' anthology *Wheels* was dedicated to Owen and contained seven of his poems — and then, in 1920, came the volume of his *Collected Poems*, edited by Siegfried Sassoon and Edith Sitwell with an introduction by Sassoon. The next significant step came in 1931 when Edmund Blunden — himself recognised and highly regarded as a poet and chronicler of the war years — published his own new and enlarged edition of Owen's poems. This included a lengthy memoir which discussed Owen's writing and presented his life through extracts from his many letters. It was this book which brought Owen clearly into focus for poets writing in the 1930s who recognised Owen as a link between the nineteenth century Romantics and their own very different ideas.

Then in 1935 C. Day Lewis was the first non-combatant poet to promote Owen's work in print, speaking in his book *A Hope for Poetry* of the Georgian poets and their place in Edwardian

The British War Graves Commission corner of Ors village cemetery. Owen's grave is third from the left in the back row.

England, followed by the drama of the First World War:

'The winds blew, the floods came... One only rode the whirlwind: Wilfred Owen, killed on the Sambre canal, spoke above the barrage and the gas-cloud, saying to us, "The poetry is in the pity".

Day Lewis wrote of Owen as an immediate ancestor of his own generation of poets; and others since then — including W. H. Auden, T. S. Eliot, Dylan Thomas, Philip Larkin, Stephen Spender and Ted Hughes — have acknowledged his importance and influence. Owen's experiments with rhyme and pararhyme gave him a technical authority among other poets which matched the general reader's instinctive response to the emotions he expressed.

In 1936 W. B. Yeats famously excluded the poets of the First World War from his selection for the *Oxford Book of Modern Verse* because 'passive suffering is not a theme for poetry'. He considered Owen 'unworthy of the poets' corner of a country newspaper' but this was controversial even at the time and in later years Owen has come to be regarded as an essential voice both of the Great War and of English poetry of the twentieth century. Literary reputations are notoriously subject to cycles of critical fashion: but it is worth noting that Owen's influence has been acknowledged more widely by each succeeding generation of readers and poets since his death. His work continues to be moving for readers of all ages; his is one of the few voices through whom we feel a genuine contact with humanity at war. This is more than simply 'reportage' — as Sassoon wrote in 1948, nearly three decades after his introduction to the 1920 volume of collected poems, Owen 'revealed how, out of realistic horror and scorn, poetry might be made'.

Day Lewis's comments were written when survivors of the Great War were still alive, but the gap between the combatant and the civilian which had so angered Sassoon, Owen and others remained. The civilian could read any number of histories and memoirs if he wanted to know the facts about the war — but if he wanted to understand this cataclysmic event in terms of human nature he must turn to poets who expressed the feelings of damaged humanity. The First World War changed English society conclusively: it is hardly surprising that it changed the national literary forms of expression too, a topic covered in detail in Paul Fussell's stimulating and influential book *The Great War and Modern Memory*.

In 1967 a bulky edition of Owen's *Collected Letters* was published, with an introduction by its editors Harold Owen and John Bell. This followed the publication earlier in the 1960s of Harold's own memoirs, *Journey from Obscurity*, a three-volume account of the Owen family's childhood years and his own career which includes a great deal about Wilfred and his development. Fascinating to read and full of vivid glimpses of the Owen family life, these memoirs have been challenged in some quarters. In the 1960s Alec Paton, Wilfred's closest friend when the two boys were pupils at Birkenhead Institute until the Owens moved to Shrewsbury in 1906, asserted that *Journey from Obscurity* should be read as fiction rather than fact, while others accepted Harold's memories and descriptions without question.

In the years before these publications Harold Owen carried out his own 'editing' of the letters, obliterating or removing words or phrases which at the time he considered ill-advised or unsuitable for wider readership. Many of these alterations seem to have been innocuous and the letters can be regarded in effect as Wilfred's 'autobiography'. Wilfred himself regarded them as a form of diary; they illuminate and explain many incidents which formed the basis for poems and, taken in conjunction with the poems, are an invaluable source of information and atmosphere.

The impression given by Harold is one of hardship in slum conditions, of gloom and an almost unrelieved struggle against poverty. Writing many years later, he quotes conversations word for word so that the various personalities emerge, particularly Wilfred, himself and their parents. Allowance should perhaps be made for the passage of time, for Susan Owen's nostalgia for her more comfortable childhood, and possibly for the resentment of a younger brother who felt disregarded while his elder brother was favoured and encouraged in every way.

Devotees of Wilfred's poetry protested against what they perceived as harsh judgement; citizens of Birkenhead protested against what they considered an unfair image of their city. As time passes the 'personality' side of the argument will diminish — except that the poet's own letters provide an invaluable background to his own character and to his poems.

Owen's development from minor adolescent romanticism to the full range and depth of his expression has been much studied and the astonishing sudden maturity of his writing in the final year of his life has frequently been compared to that of Keats. The teasing question remains, whether he would have developed his very individual poetic voice without the pressures of his war experience or if he had survived the war and become part of the literary world of the 1920s and '30s.

When the war began he was still too young, in terms of personal maturity as much as years, for us to assess what peacetime adulthood would have brought; but the intensity of his feeling allied to the technical skill based on the years of patient study make it difficult to imagine a return to his previous lush romanticism. The poverty and inequalities of the 1920s, a mockery of Lloyd George's promised 'land fit for heroes' would surely have inspired the same compassion for the social victims of the peace as the war had created for its long-suffering soldiers.

When Wilfred was an unhappy adolescent at Dunsden, the contrasts in his life were confusing and destructive; by the time he had escaped from his mother's single-minded devotion, passed through the fierce processes of war and shell-shock, through death all around him and recovery at Craiglockhart — with the crucial stimulus and support of his friendship with Sassoon —

the contrasts fused into creativity and brought a unity of purpose and determination to his instinctive voice.

Owen's voice is the urgent claim of the 'expert witness', explaining and creating sympathy in his readers through the precision and clarity of his expression. Like some modern-day war correspondent who gains authority by speaking from the heart of violence, in the human essentials of warfare he was seen to 'tell it as it was'. Equally, though he detached himself from the orthodoxies of the Church of England, his passionate belief in human spirituality underlies the intensity of his anger and compassion.

As the traditional construction of poetic expression has shifted towards less apparently rigid forms, expressed in challenging style which sometimes presents difficulties for readers, perhaps Owen's use of 'pararhyme' makes his poetry approachable for both those who dislike obvious formal rhyme schemes and those who are alarmed by lack of obvious structure in poetry. Perhaps his background and personality, for readers of biography or literary criticism, comes over as disarmingly 'ordinary'. He seems to be an acknowledged 'great poet' accessible to readers who are not particularly concerned with 'modern poetry' — yet at the same time, the makers of later twentieth century poetry have acknowledged Owen as their ancestor. In his 1965 book, *Heroes' Twilight*, Bernard Bergonzi remarks that:

> 'Within a few months he gave the poetry of the anti-heroic attitude... as absolute an expression as the traditional heroic attitude had received in countless epics and dramas of the Western tradition. And this reflected a basic change in human sensibility. ... War was no longer the same; modern technology had seen to that; and Owen ensured that it could no longer be *seen* as the same.'

Books such as Jon Stallworthy's essential biography (1974) or Dominic Hibberd's two major books on Owen and his poetry (*Owen the Poet*, 1986 and *Wilfred Owen, the Last Year*, 1992), and others, underline this unique quality of Owen and his writing: the paradox that despite the intensely felt and personal nature of his poetry Owen knew how to move outside his own personality, his separate individuality, and present human nature under the duress of intolerable circumstances. It has been suggested that Owen's impersonality and selflessness raise moral questions about the purposes of war which many people prefer to avoid.

Owen's personality continues to fascinate, however, as it has done ever since his death — not just Yeat's sour dismissal of war poetry but questions which exercised Owen during his lifetime. Was he actually accused of cowardice? He apparently thought so; in the end he felt himself redeemed by the actions which won the recommendation for the Military Cross. He saw his officially acknowledged success in battle as the vindication of his right to speak for the victims of war.

His courage and achievements as an officer, then, are no longer in any doubt, but other queries persist. One that draws a wide range of answers is the possibility that Wilfred was homosexual. Such a notion would scarcely have been conceivable in the Owen family in their quiet Shrewsbury suburb — but, although he seems to have broken away successfully in the final months of his life, the intensity of the relationship between Wilfred and his mother raises questions in a post-Freudian world; and many of the literary-minded men to whom he was turning most keenly for companionship in his last months of life were undoubtedly homosexual to a more or less obvious degree. The influence of writers such as Swinburne and Oscar Wilde (and similar French poets) can be seen in Owen's work from the time he arrived in Bordeaux. The very deep affection for such friends as Sassoon — more than was reciprocated, in fact — was a natural sequel to Owen's life-long capacity for hero worship; we do not know the contents of the material burnt by Susan after Wilfred's death but the adolescent writing that survives appears little concerned with girls or conventional love poetry. Certainly no passion equals the fury, despair and human compassion aroused by the war.

Wilfred Owen has been claimed by many people and factions as 'one of their own' — devout Christians and committed non-believers, soldiers and civilians, pacifists, hetero- and homo-sexuals, survivors of the Great War and schoolchildren of the 1990s. Among the wide range of readers who are drawn to his poems there are survivors of both World Wars and other conflicts, members of the modern armed services and scholars, readers without any academic framework, and young people who have no connection with war.

He has inspired an enormous range of creative work in all

forms of art, of which Britten's War Requiem is probably the most widely known. The War Requiem, first performed in 1962, used some of Owen's poetry within the setting of the Latin Mass for the Dead and brought Owen's depths of irony and feeling to the attention of many new readers; he is widely admired in non-English-speaking countries and his poetry is taught to students in France, Germany and Japan as well as to English and American pupils.

In the late twentieth century, views on war — and poetry — are naturally different from attitudes in earlier centuries and decades. Civilians know more about the face of war than could have been dreamed of by men in the trenches of 1914-18; and, as television and newspapers bring warfare into every household, feelings have changed about the effect of war on those involved. Wilfred Owen's phrase, 'The pity of war', represents the views of many people who do not read poetry.

Soldier/civilian, pacifist/warrior, creative artist/social conscience, he represents many attitudes and moods, interpreting each to each: this is perhaps the secret of his great appeal.

Symmetry, *the sculpture by Paul de Monchaux unveiled outside Shrewsbury Abbey in June 1993. A line from 'Strange Meeting' ('I am the enemy you killed, my friend') is engraved on one side and the design echoes the symmetries in this poem as well as the trenches of 1917 and the canal at Ors in 1918.*

Bibliography

Any general bibliography of the First World War shows a clear pattern; there is the rise and fall of memoirs and edited volumes — the novels and memoirs of experiences written by survivors in the fifteen years after 1918, thinning out until Sassoon dominates the later 1930s and the 1940s almost alone. Henry Williamson's autobiographical novels followed — but now, we have the reassessments and the scholarly critical analyses, the definitive editions of poets' work.

This new breed of expert study spreads its attention over very broad fields — the full extent of art, social and cultural history, placing the individual threads of attitude and expression into the complex tapestry of the Great War.

The bibliography prepared by David Hughes gives details and comment on many books which illustrate the growth of Owen's reputation and the general interest in the literature of the First World War. I have drawn on them in writing this book and hope that this list will help readers to extend their knowledge of Owen's work.

Books that are out of print are included to give a fuller picture and can often be found in libraries or secondhand/antiquarian book dealers.

Helen McPhail

Bibliography prepared by David Hughes

Editions of Owen and Studies of his Work

Wheels, 1919: Fourth Cycle   ed. Edith Sitwell
  B. H. Blackwell
  1919
  Simply, the first post-war publication of Owen's work: seven poems which kept him in the reader's eye until Sassoon's edition appeared (for which Edith Sitwell did the work).

Poems by Wilfred Owen   ed. & intro. Siegfried Sassoon
  Chatto and Windus
  1920   *a facsimile edition, by*
  The Imperial War Museum, Department of Printed Books
  1990   0 901627 61 5
  This facsimile reminds us (it contains just 23 poems) how much of Owen remained unpublished for how long. It is fascinating to read this text against e.g. Stallworthy's and to see how our reading of the poems has evolved. It has a modern introduction by Martin Taylor, editor of Lads (see page 78)
  1993   *reissue of the facsimile edition, by*
  The Imperial War Museum, Department of Printed Books
    •   1 870423 03 8
  Centenary edition, a limited numbered reissue with a previously unpublished tribute to Owen by Edmund Blunden.

71

The Poems of Wilfred Owen   ed. Edmund Blunden
Chatto and Windus
1931
> *The introduction/biography remains a masterpiece of its kind. This was the first lengthy edition, containing 59 poems. The texts of the poems are defective, but the whole edition is absorbing in its reminders to us who have so much available that earlier readers were very restricted indeed.*

Wilfred Owen: A Critical Study   D. S. R. Welland
Chatto and Windus
1960
1978   07011 1201 8
> *Among the earliest of the critical studies, this did a superb job of drawing attention to (while not actually answering) most of the important questions about Owen's poetry.*

The Collected Poems of Wilfred Owen   ed. & intro. C. Day Lewis
Chatto and Windus
1963   0 7011 1293 X
> *The text which restored Owen to a modern readership: Day Lewis has been superseded but his work was invaluable in widening the range of what was available and in asserting Owen's continuing value as a poet speaking to the second half of the twentieth century and beyond. Of especial importance to my own reading of Owen was Day Lewis's attention to the variety and condition of the manuscripts behind the printed poems. The order of the poems may seem curious but it is powerful, and Day Lewis brings a poet's sensitivity to the annotations.*

Wilfred Owen: Collected Letters   ed. Harold Owen and John Bell
Oxford University Press
1967
> *Harold Owen excised passages from quite a few letters in an attempt (which he later came to regret and apologise for) to sanitize his brother's reputation. Otherwise an excellent volume, sensibly but not heavily annotated and well indexed (often what matters in one's desire to relate the letters to the poems).*

Journey from Obscurity   Harold Owen
Wilfred Owen 1893-1918: Memoirs of the Owen Family
   1   Childhood   1963   0 19 211146 9
   2   Youth   1964
   3   War   1965
Oxford University Press

Aftermath   Harold Owen
Oxford University Press
1970   19 211195 7
> *In the end, all of these seem to tell us as much about Harold Owen and the rest of Wilfred's family as they do about Wilfred himself; but read in conjunction with the Letters they add up to an indispensable biography.*

Wilfred Owen: War Poems and Others   ed. & intro. Dominic Hibberd
Chatto and Windus
1973   0 7011 1989 6
An interesting selection of 56 poems, and prose printed in roughly
chronological order (broken, e.g. to place a letter next to a poem of
related interest but later composition).

Wilfred Owen: A Biography   Jon Stallworthy
Oxford University Press, and Chatto and Windus
1974   0 19 211719 X
The first full biography, containing a mass of information, is now
somewhat dated — for example it does not address the necessary
questions about Owen's homosexuality. Its best and most
innovative feature is its inclusion of photographs of many of Owen's
manuscripts, those of Anthem for Doomed Youth *being among the*
most interesting (and presented here in an arguable sequence).

Wilfred Owen's Poetry, A Study Guide   James F. McIlroy
Heinemann Educational Books
1974   0 435 18567 5
The text is specifically designed for A-level candidates, and possesses
the limitations and strengths which that implies. It should be titled
'Wilfred Owen's War Poetry'. It relates Owen to the standard 'other'
war poets adequately, and explains 32 of the poems clearly and
sensibly, if somewhat didactically.

Writers and their Work: Wilfred Owen   Dominic Hibberd
Longman, for the British Council
1975   0 582 01246 5
Like all the others in the series, this is a clear, concise introduction
to Owen and his writing. There is a good mixture of biography and
critical commentary, without any pretence to completeness.

Tradition Transformed: Studies in the Poetry of Wilfred Owen
C. W. K. Gleerup   Sven Bäckman
1979   91 40 04705 9
It can be dense reading, but more than any other this is the critical
text which I have found important in developing and stimulating
my own reading of Owen: particularly good on the literary origins
of Owen's poetry.

Wilfred Owen: The Complete Poems and Fragments
                                                        ed. Jon Stallworthy
Chatto and Windus: The Hogarth Press, and Oxford University Press
1983   0 7011 2716 3 (v.1)   0 70112717 1 (v.2)
Hideously expensive, beautifully produced edition getting as close
as contemporary knowledge and scholarship allowed to Owen's final
intentions — and if you want to disagree, the information is here
to allow you to do so. The two volumes allow poems and their
manuscripts to be read side by side.

The Poems of Wilfred Owen   ed. Jon Stallworthy
Hogarth Poetry, The Hogarth Press
1985   0 7012 1015 X
The paperback edition to possess, based on Stallworthy's own definitive Complete Poems and Fragments. *The notes explain the dating of the poems, and give a very few additional facts about them. Line notes are a bit sparse, but give helpful references or definitions while not offering suggestions for interpretations.*

Wilfred Owen: The Poems   ed. Jon Silkin
The Penguin Poetry Library
1985   0 14 058513 3
This edition was withdrawn rapidly after publication because of unresolved copyright difficulties — which is a pity, because Silkin always has important and interesting things to say about Owen.

Wilfred Owen: Selected Letters   ed. John Bell
Oxford University Press
1985   0 19 281914 3
A satisfactory paperback selection of the more important letters. Owen's correspondence is the nearest we can get to an autobiography and there is much to be learnt from them.

Owen the Poet   Dominic Hibberd
The Macmillan Press
1986   0 333 38448 2
This is a marvellous piece of scholarship, the most complete and up to date study and assessment of Owen's poetry. It is constantly informative and stimulating, never irritating, and includes a thorough bibliography. I do, however, object to the standard of production of the hardback: the paperback has been corrected.

York Notes on Selected Poems by Wilfred Owen   Benedikte Uttenthal
Longman York Press
1986   0 582 79287 8
Easily derided, this is actually one of the better volumes of 'student notes', giving sensible accounts and assessments of individual poems. Notes on textual meanings and difficulties are heavily based on Stallworthy, and are wide-ranging; while (most important) the emphasis of the whole book is on the desirability of readers forming their own readings and interpretations.

Wilfred Owen: Anthem for a Doomed Youth   Kenneth Simcox
Woburn Press
1987   0 7130 0179 8
Although I disagree with some of Simcox's assessments I value his book because it drives me to re-assess my own readings.

Wilfred Owen: Selected Poetry and Prose   ed. Jennifer Breen
Routledge English Texts
1988   0 415 00733 X
Designed 'for readers for whom the study of literature also involves the study of its historical and critical contexts'. The introduction is very helpful; the selection of poems is not restricted to the obvious 'war' ones; there is a history of each poem's publication; the notes are eclectic and informative.

Journey from Obscurity   Harold Owen
Oxford University Press
1988   0 19 2822586
*Reissue, with an introduction by John Wain, of a 1968 abridged
version of Harold Owen's three-volume memoirs. The substantial
trilogy is skilfully abridged to give the full flavour of Harold's own
life but retains a much greater proportion of his descriptions of
Wilfred. John Wain's introduction is sympathetic to both brothers.*

Wilfred Owen: The Last Year   Dominic Hibberd
Constable
1992   0 09 470820 7
*A wide-ranging, refreshing and illuminating study, drawing together
much material relating the life to the poetry, and some stimulating
re-assessments of earlier ideas.*

Wilfred Owen   Merryn Williams
Seren Books, Autumn 1993

Wilfred Owen's Voices   Douglas Kerr
Oxford University Press, Autumn 1993

Associated Material

General Introductions

Writers & Their Work, 100: War Poets, 1914-1918   Edmund Blunden
Longman, for the British Council
1958 (with additions 1964)
*Dated but interesting introductory essay on Older War Poetry, Rupert
Brooke and Others, Siegfried Sassoon and Mainly Wilfred Owen.*

Stand: The War Poets   ed. Jon Silkin
Stand, Vol. 3, No. 4
1960
*A seminal edition of the now famous literary magazine: if the
modern revival of interest in the Literature of the Great War can
be said to have a single origin, this is it. Owen is paired with Brooke
in an essay by Geoffrey Matthews.*

Poets of the First World War   Jon Stallworthy
Oxford University Press with the Imperial War Museum
1974   0 19 211847 1
*Brief accounts of the lives and works of Brooke, Blunden, Owen,
Rosenberg, Sassoon and Thomas, well illustrated and with a
facsimile manuscript from each (Anthem for Doomed Youth).*

Casebook: Poetry of the First World War   ed. Dominic Hibberd
Macmillan
1981   0 333 26121
*Three sections of important critical articles on Owen, especially
reviews of the 1920 edition of the Poems; reactions from the inter-
war years; and the 1960s increase of interest.*

The Penguin Book of First World War Prose ed. Jon Glover
Penguin & Jon Silkin
1986 0 670 80106 2
*A wide-ranging, well chosen anthology, whose contents and reading
lists will deny you the comfort of the assumption that only the
English had anything worthwhile to say about the Great War (cf.
The Penguin Book of First World War Poetry).*

Closely Associated or Influential Writers

Siegfried's Journey, 1916-1920 Siegfried Sassoon
Faber & Faber
1945
*Sassoon's autobiography of his war experience, expanded from the
fictionalised accounts of The Complete Memoirs of George Sherston
(cf.). It contains the classic account of Owen's meeting with Sassoon
at Craiglockhart War Hospital, which so influenced Owen's poetry,
and Sassoon's friendship with, and support of, Owen and his
reputation thereafter. The account is open to dispute, but is essential
to give an idea of Owen's impact on those who knew him as a poet
while he was alive.*

Collected Poems 1908-1956 Siegfried Sassoon
Faber and Faber
1961
*The Poems of The Old Huntsman, which so excited Owen as to
induce him to ask for Sassoon's autograph at Craiglockhart, leading
to their meetings and friendship. See the Collected Letters for Owen's
reactions and an indication of the poems' and their author's
influence.*

Siegfried Sassoon: The War Poems arr. Rupert Hart-Davis
Faber and Faber
1983 0 571 13015 1
*The same, but in order of composition rather than original printing;
with some editorial and authorial notes; and with a few previously
uncollected or unpublished.*

Siegfried Sassoon: Diaries 1920-1922 ed. Rupert Hart-Davis
Faber & Faber
1981 0 571 11685 X
*A sporadic account of Sassoon's work in publishing Owen and of
his relations with Wilfred's brother Harold (cf. Aftermath).*

Siegfried Sassoon: Diaries 1915-1918 ed. Rupert Hart-Davis
Faber & Faber
1983 0 571 11997 2
*An interesting illumination of the later accounts Sassoon gave of
his meetings with — and friendship with — Owen: it is clear that
Sassoon's later high opinion of Owen did not begin immediately.
It may be particularly significant that the diaries dealing with the
actual Craiglockhart period were not among those given to Hart-
Davis, and he has had to fill the gap from other sources.*

Goodbye to All That   Robert Graves
Jonathan Cape
1929
Cassell (revised with new Prologue & Epilogue)
1957
A prose treatment of Graves' experiences during the Great War: its accounts are fictionalised beyond the point of reliability, but they did form opinion (cf. In Broken Images); and this version of Graves' early reactions to Owen is therefore important.

In Broken Images: Selected Letters of Robert Graves 1914-1946
Hutchinson   ed. Paul O'Prey
1982   0 09 147720 4
Important in understanding how Owen was originally received by those whom he came to consider his peers.

Robert Graves: His Life and Work   Martin Seymour-Smith
Abacus
1983   0 349 13237 2
Interesting sidelights on Owen from the point of view of someone regarded as one of the other major poets of the time.

Under Fire: The Story of a Squad   Henri Barbusse
Ernest Flammarion (Paris, 1916)
Dent 1917; Everyman Library 1926   trans. Fitzwater Wray
Perhaps the first realistic novel of the war, read by both Owen and Sassoon (who showed it to Owen at Craiglockhart): essential reading if you are to understand one of the origins of Owen's poetic style and subject matter.

Owen and Barbusse and Fitzwater Wray   Jon Glover
(article in) Strand Magazine Vol. 21, No. 2
1980
The article examines the influence of Under Fire *on Owen.*

Related Anthologies and Collections

Georgian Poetry   ed. James Reeves
Penguin
1962
Anthology re-habilitating poetry of the reign of King George V, not confined to work published in Marsh's annual collections but reviving an interesting variety: 12 poems from Owen; others from W. H. Davies, Housman, Hodgson, Young, Brooke, etc: worth browsing for a flavour of the times.

Up the Line to Death: The War Poets, 1914-1918   ed. Brian Gardner
Methuen
1964 (revised 1976)   0 417 02350 2
If one anthology can be said to have revived interest in the poetry of the Great War, this is it. Although it is now dated in both its selection of poems and its account of them, it is important to know the way many of our views of the poets and their poems were formed.

The Penguin Book of First World War Poetry

ed. & intro. Jon Silkin

Penguin
1979   0 14 042255 2

*This idiosyncratic anthology, particularly in its introduction,
contains an important, controversial discussion of Owen's work,
focussing particularly on* Strange Meeting. *It is essential reading.
The anthology itself contains 18 Owen poems, including a version
of the manuscript of* Strange Meeting *which discusses the status of
the commonly accepted text. See also* The Penguin Book of First
World War Prose.

The English Poets of the First World War   John Lehmann

Thames & Hudson
1981   0 500 01256 3

*This well illustrated narrative account of the poets touches on some
of those not normally included in such books, giving few but well-
chosen poems and an intelligent critical commentary.*

Scars Upon My Heart   ed. Catherine Reilly

Virago
1981   0 860068 226 9

*A salutary lesson in getting rid of pre-conceptions about 'Poetry of
the Great War': read it.*

Poetry of the Great War, An Anthology   ed. Hibberd & Onions

Macmillan
1986   0 333 36219 5

*Excellent anthology, showing poetry's development during the war,
contradicting the view that it moved smoothly from enthusiasm
(Brooke) to protest (Sassoon) and elegy (Owen).*

The War Poets   Robert Giddings

Bloomsbury
1988   07475 0145 9

*An over-view of the poetry of the Great War: it is a clever, inclusive
text, quoting adequate numbers of poems and placing them in a
clearly narrated context. Owen's story is interwoven with those of
the other important poets, giving particular attention to Graves and
Sassoon.*

Lads: Love Poetry of the Trenches   ed. Martin Taylor

Constable
1989   0 09 468830 3

*A well selected anthology illustrating the thesis that 'the affection
between fighting men went beyond the bounds of ordinary
comradeship. Much of the poetry of the trenches is characterized
by a strong homo-erotic element. Owen is given much attention.*